THE ATTRIBUTES OF GOD IN PAULINE THEOLOGY

A Dissertation

Presented to

the Faculty of the Department of Systematic Theology

Dallas Theological Seminary

by

William Delane Thrasher

August 1982

Wipf and Stock Publishers

150 West Broadway • Eugene OR 97401

2001

The Attributes of God in Pauline Theology

By Thrasher, William

ISBN: 1-57910-736-2

Printed by *Wipf and Stock Publishers*
150 West Broadway • Eugene OR 97401

THE ATTRIBUTES OF GOD

IN PAULINE THEOLOGY

William Delane Thrasher, Th.D.

The aim of this dissertation is to present Paul's doctrine of the attributes of God. While some writers have noted the importance of this doctrine in Paul's thinking, it has been virtually ignored in works dealing with Pauline theology.

The method of the study is the discipline of Biblical Theology as it has been defined by Ryrie and Ladd. This method is applied to this important doctrine, and the result is the development of Paul's treatment of the attributes of God.

The attributes of God that are discussed are those which naturally flow out of an inductive study of the sources of Pauline theology. This study has included the thirteen letters of the New Testament which claim Pauline authorship as well as the speeches of Paul in Acts as its sources for Paul's thought. These perfections are presented under the categories of God's intellectual, moral, volitional, and constitutional attributes. A final chapter also discusses the development of the idea of the glory of God in Paul's writings.

The discussion of God's knowledge and wisdom considers their lexical basis, the manner in which Paul describes these attributes, and the particular ways in which the apostle noted their display in his life and thinking. Paul's contrast of God's wisdom to the wisdom of the world is also developed.

The moral attributes of God that can be clearly seen include the truths of God's love, mercy, grace, kindness, patience, truthfulness and faithfulness, righteousness, and wrath. In addition to the discussion of their lexical basis, the Pauline development of each of these attributes is presented with special attention given to their display in Christ.

The truths of God's sovereignty and power are presented next in the dissertation. The Pauline concepts that relate to God's sovereignty are predestination, foreknowledge, election, calling, purpose, will, and kingdom. These are developed both lexically and thematically as the foundational nature of God's sovereignty is observed in Paul's thinking. The presentation of God's power deals with the various word groups in Paul that denote this attribute, the supremacy of God's power, and its relationship to the other attributes. The contrast in Paul's writing between God's power and man's weakness is also noted, as well as the various ways God has displayed His power.

The last group of attributes to be considered includes God's eternality, immortality, incorruptibility, life, invisibility, and omnipresence. The lexical basis and meaning of each is set forth with special emphasis upon their bearing on Paul's life.

The final topic that is treated is the glory of God. The lexical basis draws special attention to the relationship of δόξα to כבוד. The development of this idea focuses upon God's glory in Christ and the responsibility of man to glorify God.

TABLE OF CONTENTS

CHAPTER I

INTRODUCTION

The Importance of the Study

Importance of the doctrine of God in Pauline theology

The doctrine of God is a central feature of Pauline theology.[1] While it is not the burden of this study to argue for the controlling thought in Paul's mind, this assertion at the very least shows the importance of the doctrine to Pauline theology.[2] In fact, Ramsey states, "Probably no one will hesitate as to what was the foundational principle in the thought of Paul. His whole mind was built on the foundation: God is."[3] Ridderbos[4] devotes some time in discussing Paul's theocentric view of sanctification, and more recently, Beker[5] argues for Paul's theocentric outlook. The following observations, likewise, have as their purpose to show the importance of this doctrine to Pauline theology.

It is in Paul's writings that one reads not only of God's desire to proclaim His name throughout the whole earth and to make known the riches of His glory (Rom. 9:17, 23), but also that the praise of His glory is the designed end of all His work (Eph. 1:12, 14) and especially the praise of His grace (Eph. 1:6, 2:7). In Pauline thought it is not man who is exalted, for the ways and works of God exclude human boasting (Rom. 3:27, 4:2, 11:32; 1 Cor. 1:29) and have as their climax "that God may be all in all" (1 Cor. 15:28).

In addition to the general observations of the above paragraph, the importance of the doctrine of God can be seen in the life and ministry of the apostle, the Christian ministry in general, the doctrine of the church, and in the doctrine of man. In regard to the life and ministry of Paul, it is only in the context of the sovereign will of God that his conversion and apostleship are considered (Gal. 1:13-16, Eph. 1:1); and it is only the enablement of God that provided his adequacy for the ministry (2 Cor. 3:5). His plans and ambitions were always subject to the will of God (Acts 18:21; Rom. 1:10; 1 Cor. 4:19, 16:7), and he found his identity in being a bondservant of God (Gal. 1:10, Phil. 1:1, Titus 1:1). When he reported his accomplishments it was a report of what God had done in him and through him (Acts 14:27, 15:4; Rom. 15:18; 1 Cor. 15:10). In regard to the Christian ministry in general, not only was it God who authored the work of salvation (2 Cor. 5:18), reconciled the world (2 Cor. 5:19), and committed to man the word of reconciliation (2 Cor. 5:19); but also it was God who produced the effects in people's lives (1 Cor. 3:6-7), even though it is proper to speak of ministers as God's fellow workers (1 Cor. 3:9). In relation to the doctrine of the church, only Paul uses the phrase "church of God" (1 Cor. 1:2; 10:32; 11:16, 22; 15:9; 2 Cor. 1:1; Gal. 1:13; 1 Thess. 2:14; 2 Thess. 1:4; 1 Tim.

3:5, 15). Perhaps the importance of the doctrine of God is seen nowhere as clearly as in the doctrine of man. As Stacey has said, "Paul looked to God first and then considered man as he stood in divine light."[6] In Pauline theology the glory of man is that he is the image and glory of God (1 Cor. 11:7), and the glory of the new man is that he is being renewed in that image (Col. 3:10). Paul's concern for man was that he not worship an unknown God. In this regard, Paul sought to correct any false idea of the divine nature (Acts 17:23, 29). His concern and prayer for believers was that they constantly increase in their knowledge of God (Col. 1:10). While other examples might be cited, the above evidence is sufficient to see that "the entire Pauline system seems to be rooted and grounded in the apostle's conception of God."[7]

Neglect of the doctrine of God in works dealing with Pauline theology

Bultmann begins his study of Paul's theology with the statement that "every assertion about God is simultaneously an assertion about man and vice versa."[8] However, as Moxnes has contended, the outcome of Bultmann's statement was a one-sided concentration on man.[9] Morgan, likewise, accuses Bultmann of making anthropology central and neglecting the basic foundation of the doctrine of God.[10] Stevens expresses his concern in the following manner:

> The apostle's conception of God is developed quite incidentally, and has commonly received no separate treatment by writers on biblical theology. But this conception is of first importance for Paul's doctrinal system and is deserving of careful elucidation; for it is in the thought of God that the plan of grace for sinners must arise, and it must be executed in accordance with his fixed purpose.[11]

Dahl states that "for more than a generation the majority of New Testament scholars have not only eliminated direct references to God from their works, but also neglected detailed and comprehensive investigation of statements about God."[12] The same author expresses his concern by noting, "Whereas a number of major works and monographs deal with the Christology--or ecclesiology, eschatology, etc.--of the New Testament; it is hard to find any comprehensive or penetrating study of the theme'God in the New Testament.'"[13]

At least some of the reason for this neglect in New Testament theology and especially Pauling theology is due to the incidental development of the doctrine. However, these incidental references to God in Paul's writing show the way in which it permeated his thought. Weidner expresses this point:

> When we take into consideration that the Apostle speaks of these attributes of God only in the course of developing and expounding other doctrines, each of these utterances gain a peculiar life and force. These truths, in Paul's estimation, appear not as worn out coins, but fresh from the mint evidences of a living faith, clearly imprinted.[14]

Also the incidental development of the doctrine of God does not mean that the data is insufficient to gain accurate insight into God's character. Speaking not only for Pauline theology but for the entire New Testament, Guthrie writes, "Anyone who seeks an answer to the question, 'What is the God of the NT like?', will find no formal statements, but a mass of incidental indications, which nevertheless are invaluable in throwing light on many facets of the character of God."[15]

The Method of the Study

Biblical Theology described

Biblical Theology is defined by Ryrie as "that branch of theological science which deals systematically with the historically conditioned progress of the self-revelation of God as deposited in the Bible."[16] Ladd writes that "Biblical theology is that discipline which sets forth the message of the books of the Bible in their historical setting."[17] At least three key elements should be noted in regard to this discipline. First, it is systematic in the sense that "Biblical theology attempts to bring the contents of the Bible to a greater degree of systemization than is found immediately in the Bible itself."[18] Secondly, it is sensitive to the fact that God has progressively revealed Himself. In this regard "Biblical theology does justice to the requirements of exegesis in context and also to the inner complexity of the Scripture in their progressive historical connection with the unfolding redemptive plan of God."[19] In other words, Biblical Theology deals with God's revelation in the Bible in its historical setting. Thirdly, it is biblical in that "its source of doctrine is the Bible."[20] As Ryrie notes, "this is not to rule out the use of historical facts which may come from other sources, but it is to affirm that the doctrine to be systematized is found in the words of the Bible."[21] Also the doctrine of the Bible is set forth in "its own terms, categories, and thought forms."[22]

After noting these central elements of Biblical Theology, a brief note should be made in regard to its relationship to Systematic Theology. It is appropriate to state that "Biblical Theology is foundational to Systematic Theology."[23] While the latter considers all forms of God's revelation, "the principal source of revelation is Holy Scripture."[24] Murray also refers to the foundational nature of Biblical Theology when he writes:

> Systematic theology deals with special revelation as a finished product incorporated for us in Holy Scripture. But special revelation in its totality is never properly conceived of apart from the history by which it became a finished product. As we think of, study, appreciate, appropriate, and apply the revelation put in our possession by inscripturation, we do not properly engage in any of these exercises except as the panorama of God's movements in history comes within our vision or at least forms the background of our thought.[25]

This same writer summarizes this thought in the following manner, "Therefore, what is the special interest of biblical theology is never divorced from our thought when we study any part of Scripture and seek to bring its treasures of truth to bear upon the synthesis which systematic theology aims to accomplish."[26]

The relationship between these two disciplines can also be seen in the service that each can provide for the other. Biblical Theology not only provides a foundation for Systematic Theology but also can serve to show the unity of the message of Scripture, which is necessary in order to do Systematic Theology. "Orthodox Systematic theology rests on the premise of the unity of Scripture, the consent of all its parts."[27] Ryrie speaks of this relationship between Biblical and Systematic Theology when he writes:

> This higher unity perceived by the method of Biblical Theology proves the validity of the doctrines of Systematic Theology, for if the teachings of the various writers of the New Testament only contained a conglomeration of human opinions which were found often to be contradictory, there would be no true dogmatics. The cardinal doctrines of God, Christ, sin, salvation, the Church, and the future are consistently and harmoniously presented by the writers.[28]

In relation to this same idea Murray observes, "Revelation is seen to be an organism and the discrete parts, or preferably phases, are perceived to be not sporadic, unrelated, and disjointed oracles, far less heterogeneous and contradictory elements, but the multiform aspects of God's intervention and self-disclosure, organically knit together and compacted, expressive not only of his marvelous grace but of the order which supreme wisdom designed."[29]

It is also correct to speak of the service that Systematic Theology provides for Biblical Theology. Biblical Theology cannot totally ignore the results of Systematic Theology. While an accurate interpretation of the total message of Scripture must consider the contribution of all the facets of truth that have been set forth by Biblical Theology, the interpretation of the various facets of God's revelation can be aided by the view of the totality of God's revelation. The hermeneutical principle, the analogy of Scripture, affirms that there is a unity to the message of God's revelation.[30] It is for this reason that Shedd writes that Systematic Theology can serve to balance and correct Biblical Theology.[31] Systematic Theology does have the advantage of speaking from the viewpoint of the whole of God's revelation and not just a portion of it.[32] This service is abused when the results of Systematic Theology are prematurely imposed upon the discipline of Biblical Theology so as to stifle the contribution of the diverse elements that compose the unified message of revelation.

Biblical Theology methodology applied

The method of Biblical Theology is applied to the subject matter of this study. A closer look at the subject matter is in order before commenting further on the methodology. The works of God are only to be considered as they clarify and illustrate the display of the attributes of God. Also, the study is not primarily concerned with the distinct Persons of the Godhead or the development of Paul's doctrine of the Trinity. At this point it should be stated that Paul's Trinitarian perspective is clear from his writings. As Lehman states, one is able to "note three elements: first, the personal distinction of the Father, the Son, and the Holy

Spirit; second, the ascription of deity to each of the three; and third, the oneness of the Godhead which underlies monotheism."[33] Lehman's list of significant references to the Trinity in Pauline theology includes Romans 7:4-6, 8:1-17, 15:15-20, 30; 1 Corinthians 2:1-5, 3:9-17, 12:3-12; 2 Corinthians 1:18-22, 3:3-6, 5:1-10, 13:14; Galatians 4:4-7; Ephesians 2:17-22, 3:14-19, 4:4-6; Colossians 1:3-8; and Titus 3:4-6.[34] To this list one might add Romans 5:1-5, 14:17-18, 15:30; 1 Corinthians 6:11, 15-20; Galatians 3:11-14; Ephesians 1:13-14, 5:18-20; Philippians 3:3; Colossians 1:6-8; 1 Thessalonians 5:18-19; and 2 Thessalonians 2:13-14. However, the scope of this study is not concerned with the development of Paul's Trinitarian perspective but rather with the one divine nature that all three Persons of the Trinity share.

The title of this dissertation contains the words "attributes of God" because "the attributes of God are those distinguishing characteristics of the divine nature."[35] The attributes of God are the "essential qualities of God"[36] in which God has both revealed Himself and by which He can be identified.

In relationship to this topic the methodology of Biblical Theology has been applied. It is, therefore, not a complete study in Pauline theology but a study in one vital area of Pauline theology. In discussing the application of the method of Biblical Theology, the three key elements that have been cited will be considered again. First, it is systematic in that the results that have been stated and developed in this study are exhibited in a more systematic form than is immediately found in Paul's writing. Secondly, an attempt has been made to be sensitive to Paul's treatment of this vital area. As Anderson writes, "Biblical theology seeks to exegete and present that which each inspired Bible writer is himself <u>in situ</u> presenting."[37] For this reason special care has been taken to look at the lexical basis for each attribute. The importance of this in relationship to Biblical Theology has been stated in the following manner:

> The great concepts which gather around key words may be grasped only by studying all the connotations which such words have and also the distinctions which they bear and develop in the use of individual authors and in the historical completion of revelation. Such inductive-historical word studies constitute the core of Biblical theology, reaching downwards into the particulars of exegesis, and upwards into the articulation of Biblical concepts together into the full scope of revealed truth.[38]

The division of the attributes that is found in this dissertation has been employed simply as a means to best exhibit the findings based on the inductive study of the sources of Pauline theology. Thirdly, the scope of revelation that is considered is limited to Pauline theology. The sources of Pauline theology includes the thirteen letters of the New Testament which claim Pauline authorship--Romans, 1 and 2 Corinthians, Galatians, Ephesians, Philippians, Colossians, 1 and 2 Thessalonians, 1 and 2 Timothy, Titus, and Philemon--as well as the speeches of Paul in Acts. In regard to the thirteen letters, nine are generally accepted and "the main current critical discussion as to Pauline authorship centers on the letter to the Ephesians and the so-called Pastoral Epistles to Timothy and Titus."[39] The objections to Pauline authorship of these four letters have been sufficiently answered[40] and "there are good reasons for accepting the thirteen letters of the New Testament which claim to have been written by Paul as being authentic."[41] While some, such as Kummel,[42] reject Paul's speeches in the Book of Acts as reliable sources for Pauline theology, "there is room for the historian to use Acts with confidence"[43] and to accept them as a source for Pauline theology as Ryrie does.[44]

Notes

[1]Ryrie maintains that the doctrine of God is the central doctrine of Pauline theology. Charles C. Ryrie, *Biblical Theology of the New Testament*, p. 203.

[2]For a list of some of the controlling thoughts that various writers have proposed see Chester K. Lehman, *Biblical Theology*, 2 vols., 2:279.

[3]W. M. Ramsay, *The Teaching of Paul in Terms of the Present Day*, p. 65.

[4]Herman Ridderbos, *Paul--An Outline of His Theology*, pp. 258-65.

[5]J. Christian Beker, *Paul the Apostle: The Triumph of God in Life and Thought*.

[6]W. D. Stacey, *The Pauline View of Man*, p. 144.

[7]Ryrie, p. 220.

[8]Rudolph Bultmann, *Theology of the New Testament*, 2 vols., 1:191.

[9]Halvor Moxnes, *Theology in Conflict: Studies in Paul's Understanding of God in Romans*, p. 4.

[10]R. Morgan, *The Nature of New Testament Theology*, p. 37.

[11]George Barker Stevens, *The Pauline Theology--A Study of the Origins and Correlation of the Doctrinal Teaching of the Apostle Paul*, p. 96.

[12]Nils Alstrop Dahl, "The Neglected Factor in New Testament Theology," *Reflection* 73 (November 1975):5.

[13]Ibid.

[14]Revere Franklin Weidner, *Biblical Theology of the New Testament*, 2 vols., 2:89.

[15]Donald Guthrie, *New Testament Theology*, pp. 89-90.

[16]Ryrie, p. 12.

[17]George Eldon Ladd, A Theology of the New Testament, p. 25.

[18]Encyclopedia of Christianity, s.v. "Biblical Theology," by Francis I. Anderson, 2:64.

[19]Ibid., 2:66. [20]Ryrie, p. 14.

[21]Ibid. [22]Ladd, p. 25.

[23]Ryrie, p. 17. Systematic Theology is defined by Chafer as "the collecting, scientifically arranging, comparing, exhibiting, and defending of all facts from any and every source concerning God and His works." Lewis Sperry Chafer, Systematic Theology, 8 vols., vol. 1: Prolegomena--Bibliology--Theology Proper, p. 6.

[24]John Murray, "Systematic Theology," The Westminster Theological Journal 26 (November 1963-May 1964):33.

[25]Ibid., p. 45. [26]Ibid., p. 45.

[27]Ibid. [28]Ryrie, p. 366.

[29]Murray, p. 46. [30]Ibid., p. 45.

[31]William G. T. Shedd, Dogmatic Theology, 3 vols., 1:13.

[32]The advantage of Systematic Theology is also that it employs the results of Historical Theology. For a discussion of the relevance of the results of Historical Theology as found in the Creeds see Bruce A. Demarest, "Christendom's Creeds: Their Relevance in the Modern World," Journal of Evangelical Theological Society 21 (December 1978):345-56.

[33]Lehman, 2:395. For a look at the monotheism in Paul see Charles H. Giblin, "Three Monotheistic Texts in Paul," Catholic Biblical Quarterly 37 (October 1975):527-47. The oneness of God is also seen in Galatians 3:20 and 1 Corinthians 8:5. The use of μόνος in Romans 16:27, 1 Timothy 1:17, and 1 Timothy 6:15-16 also is relevant to Paul's monotheism.

[34]Lehman, 2:397.

[35]Augustus H. Strong, Systematic Theology, p. 244.

[36]Shedd, 1:334.

[37]Encyclopedia of Christianity, s.v. "Biblical Theology," by Francis I. Anderson, 2:63.

[38]Ibid., 2:67-68.

[39]Richard N. Longenecker, _The Ministry and Message of Paul_, p. 16.

[40]Donald Guthrie, _New Testament Introduction_, pp. 479-508; 584-622.

[41]Longenecker, p. 17.

[42]Werner George Kümmel, _The Theology of the New Testament_, p. 140.

[43]Longenecker, p. 16.

[44]Ryrie, _Biblical Theology_, p. 164.

CHAPTER II

INTELLECTUAL ATTRIBUTES IN PAULINE THEOLOGY

The Knowledge of God

Lexical basis

Of the various words that comprise the Pauline vocabulary of knowledge, the usages of these words which denote God as the knower are really few in number. Γινώσκω is found 221 times in the New Testament and 50 of these uses are in Paul.[1] However, in only five of these uses is God the subject of the verb (1 Cor. 2:11, 3:20, 8:3; Gal. 4:9; 2 Tim. 2:19). In three of these cases the reference is to God's "loving, electing knowledge of man"[2] (1 Cor. 8:3; Gal. 4:9; 2 Tim. 2:19). This is the sense that ἐπιγινώσκω carries the one time that God is the subject of this verb in 1 Corinthians 13:12.[3] Here, the compound form does probably have an intensive force and stresses the idea of completeness.[4] This use of γινώσκω is reflective of the use of the word for ידע in the LXX. The use of γινώσκω in 1 Corinthians 3:20 simply refers to God's absolute and complete knowledge.[5] The other use of the verb in relation to God's knowledge is in 1 Corinthians 2:11 where it refers to the interaction of knowledge within the Godhead. Γνῶσις is used of God's knowledge in Romans 11:33 where it refers to His comprehensive knowledge of all things and, as Cranfield notes, perhaps includes His electing love.[6]

Οἶδα is used five times to refer to God knowing something (Rom. 8:27; 2 Cor. 11:11, 31, 12:2-3). In relation to God it refers to His absolute knowledge.[7] In classical Greek οἶδα referred to the possession of knowledge and γινώσκω referred to the acquisition of knowledge. Οἶδα referred to a complete and final knowledge while γινώσκω referred to an incomplete and developing knowledge. Οἶδα referred to a knowledge that was grasped directly or intuitively and γινώσκω referred to a knowledge that was grasped by experience, studying, or observation. It is generally agreed that this classical distinction is not always maintained in Koine Greek but as Burdick points out, "Οἶδα is the verb that most naturally would be employed to describe God's knowledge when the classical distinction is being maintained."[8] Burdick notes that "because He is omniscient, God needs no intermediate means to gain knowledge of a fact."[9] Γινώσκω is used to speak of God's special relational knowledge in Paul (1 Cor. 2:11, 8:3; Gal. 4:9; 2 Tim. 2:19) and the possible exception of 1 Corinthians 3:20 is probably due to the fact that it is a quote from the LXX.[10] Of lexical significance is also the use of μάρτυς in relation to God's knowledge in Romans 1:9, 2 Corinthians 1:23, Philippians 1:8, 1 Thessalonians 2:5, and 2:10.

Description of God's knowledge

"Oh, the depth of the riches both of the wisdom and knowledge of God" (Rom. 11:33). The apostle employs the phrase "the depths of the riches" to express his wonder and awe at the knowledge of God. While some[11] connect βάθος with the three following genitives, it is best to connect it only with πλούτου.[12] The two following genitives define the "riches," which carries the meaning of abundance.[13] It is not uncommon for Paul to use the term "riches" to speak of the riches of some attribute of God or of His glory (Rom. 2:4, 9:23; Eph. 1:7, 2:7, 3:16). Therefore, "the tautology of the phrase 'depth of the riches' is explained by the great emphasis and wonder in the mind of the writer."[14] It is in this manner that Paul describes the knowledge of God, which refers to "God's all-inclusive and exhaustive cognition and understanding."[15] It is God's knowledge that provides the means that wisdom needs. Both are viewed as the basis for His judgments or decisions and His ways or dealings with men, which are described as unsearchable and unfathomable.

In describing the knowledge of God, Paul quotes Isaiah 40:13 in 1 Corinthians 2:16 and in Romans 11:34. In quoting the LXX, he omits the middle clause in 1 Corinthians 2:16--καὶ τίς αὐτοῦ σύνβουλος ἐγένετο. The clause is retained in Romans 11:34 while the phrase ὃς συνβιβάσει αὐτόν is omitted. The question that occurs in both passages is τίς γὰρ ἔγνω νοῦν κυρίου. The purpose of the quotation in

1 Corinthians 2:16 is to give a proof--γάρ--of why no one can appraise a spiritual man. The reasoning of the apostle takes the following form. "No one can instruct the Lord. We have the mind of the Lord. Therefore, no one can instruct or judge us."[16] In Romans 11:34 it is used to substantiate Paul's exclamation concerning God's knowledge and wisdom and the unsearchable and unfathomable nature of God's judgments and ways.

In light of the answers that the questions anticipate, Paul is affirming that "no man can plumb the depths of God's mind" and that "no man can put him right."[17] "'To know the Lord's mind' is to know its contents, its plans, and its purposes."[18] While the apostle maintains that God has revealed His mind through the Spirit (1 Cor. 2:10-13) and has given the spiritual man the capacity to appraise all things (1 Cor. 2:15-16), the superiority of God's knowledge is always maintained in Paul's writings (Rom. 11:33-34). God's knowledge is independent of man but man's knowledge is dependent on God. No one can serve as God's counselor or instructor for He is omniscient.[19] God has no need to learn and is not surprised by a new discovery for His knowledge is eternal.

The knowledge of God is also described as full and complete in comparison to man's knowledge which is only partial (1 Cor. 13:9, 12). While Paul is free to admit his ignorance on a specific matter, he confidently affirms God's knowledge (2 Cor. 12:2-3).

God's knowledge is described with awe and amazement for it is the basis of His unsearchable judgments and unfathomable ways (Rom. 11:33). It is also described as independent of man's knowledge, while man's knowledge is dependent on God's revelation (Rom. 11:34; 1 Cor. 2:16). It is further described as full and complete in comparison to man's partial knowledge (1 Cor. 13:9, 12).

Contents of God's knowledge

In addition to a description of God's knowledge, the apostle also ennumerates some of its specific contents. The major emphasis is on God's knowledge of the thoughts of man. What is hidden to man is clearly seen and known by God.

The general assertion that man is fully known by God is found in 1 Corinthians 13:12. The specifics of this assertion are found in Paul's free quotation from the LXX of Psalm 94:11 as he writes, "The Lord knows the reasonings of the wise, that they are useless" (1 Cor. 3:20). God has complete knowledge of the thoughts of man and on the basis of this knowledge He also evaluates these thoughts. The same idea is found in Romans 8:27 where God is described as "He who searches the hearts." This is a common idea in the Old Testament as "to search the heart is the prerogative of God, as it implies omniscience"[20] (cf. 1 Sam. 16:7; Ps. 7:9, 139:23; Prov. 15:11; Jer. 17:10). It is because of this knowledge of the heart that Paul appeals to God as a witness to prove the truthfulness of his affirmations when no other witnesses are available or qualified. He is confident of God's full knowledge of his intercessary prayer life (Rom. 1:9), the motives of his heart (2 Cor. 1:23; 1 Thess. 2:5), his love for others (Phil. 1:8), and his behavior in the ministry (1 Thess. 2:4, 10).

God's knowledge of believers also includes His election and personal relation with them. This revolves around Paul's use of γινώσκω in such passages as 1 Corinthians 8:3, Galatians 4:9, and 2 Timothy 2:19.[21] His personal knowledge of believers involves not merely a theoretical knowledge but a knowledge that implies concern and which takes into account the limits of each individual believer in His providential dealings with them (1 Cor. 10:13; cf. Rom. 8:28).

The apostle also makes clear from his writing that God has a knowledge of the future. This is evident from his references to prophecies that have already been fulfilled (cf. Acts 13:32-37) and his teaching concerning the future for the church, for Israel, and for the world.[22] In relation to the content of God's knowledge, the contribution of Romans 8:27 should also briefly be cited. In addition to referring to God as "He who searches the heart," this verse states that the Father knows the mind of the Spirit. This in conjunction with 1 Corinthians 2:11, which states that "the thoughts of God no one knows except the Spirit of God," shows the interaction of perfect and complete knowledge within the Godhead.

Display of God's knowledge

The display of this attribute is clearly seen in Paul's life. It was comforting for Paul to appeal to God's knowledge of his love for the Corinthians (2 Cor. 11:11) and his truthfulness in his writing to them (2 Cor. 1:23; cf. Gal. 1:20). It was common for him in his ministry to maintain that God is his witness (Rom. 1:9; Phil. 1:8; 1 Thess. 2:5, 10) or to call upon God to be his witness (2 Cor. 1:23). In the apostle's unceasing prayer life (1 Thess. 1:2-3, 5:17) he knew that God knew both his needs and trials and the needs and trials of the people for which he prayed and this prompted his honest communication with God (cf. Phil. 4:6). He, likewise, was comforted that God knew his past and he did not try to hide it (1 Cor. 15:9; Gal. 1:13-14; 1 Tim. 1:12-16) and neither did he let it hinder his present pursuits (Phil. 3:13-14). He realized that God knew the opposition of believers (2 Tim. 3:12) as well as their inadequacy (2 Cor. 3:5). However, while this knowledge of God was a source of assurance and comfort to the apostle, it was a threat to those who did not comply with the gospel message for Paul maintained that "God will judge the secrets of men through Christ Jesus" (Rom. 2:16).

The display of this attribute is also seen in the fact that the reference point of all evaluation in Paul's thought is the God of perfect knowledge. Paul wrote of being holy and blameless "before Him" (Eph. 1:4; Col. 1:22) and of a justification "in His sight" (Rom. 3:20). Paul marveled that he had been justified by God; because the God who justified him was an omniscient God, who even knew the sins of his heart. Likewise, it was not others or himself who was the final judge of his life and ministry, but it was the Lord's examination that was in the forefront of his mind (1 Cor. 4:3-4).

It is also noteworthy to mention the reference to the knowledge of God in Colossians 3:10 where the goal (εἰς) of the renewal of the new self is said to be "knowledge." This knowledge is in accordance with the image of God. Ἐπίγνωσις does carry an intensive meaning as compared with γνῶσις. While the latter is concerned with the understanding of facts, the former refers to a "fuller, clearer, and more thorough knowledge."[23] It involves a knowledge and insight into the facts[24] and a spiritual perception.[25] The new self is being renewed according to the image of God "so as to be like God."[26] The special feature of that image which is selected by the apostle is knowledge. The believer is to become like God in his spiritual knowledge, insight, and perception. "There are, it is true, many points in which our relative knowledge shall never, and can never, resemble the absolute Divine omniscience."[27]

The Wisdom of God

The lexical basis

The lexical basis for this attribute centers around Paul's use of σοφία. In classical Greek σοφία referred to a skill in a certain handcraft or art, skill in daily living in the sense of sound judgment, and also was used of theoretical knowledge.[28] In the LXX σοφία is used some 138 times and 127 of these times it is used for חכמה.[29] It is the use of σοφία in the LXX that gave it its clear association with God. Wisdom is that quality which uniquely belongs to God (Job 12:13; Dan. 2:20) and the Messiah (Isa. 11:2; cf. 2 Sam. 14:20) and which was employed in His work of creation (Job 38:37; Ps. 104:24; Prov. 3:19; Jer. 10:12). God is regarded as the only true source of wisdom (Job 28:20, 23) and wisdom is seen as His gift to man (1 Kings 4:29; 2 Chron. 2:12). While wisdom may refer to the ability to do skillful work, this ability is also seen as a gift of God (Exod. 31:3, 35:31, 36:1). The beginning of wisdom for man is the fear of God (Job 28:28; Prov. 9:10). Wisdom is vitally connected with the obedience to God's revelation which was to mark Israel out as distinct from all the other nations of the world and their wisdom (Deut. 4:5-6; cf. Isa. 29:14; Jer. 50:35, 51:57).

In the New Testament σοφία "is never ascribed to anyone but God and good men, except in a plainly ironical sense."[30] The use of σοφία to denote the wisdom of God or

Christ is predominantly Pauline (1 Cor. 1:21, 24, 30; 2:7; Eph. 3:10). It is used in this way outside of Paul's writing, in Luke 11:49, Revelation 5:12, and 7:12.[31] The adjective σοφός is ascribed to God in Romans 16:27. The verb σοφίζω occurs once in Paul's writing to denote that the Scriptures impart the wisdom to man that leads to salvation (2 Tim. 3:15). The uses of σοφία in Paul is further developed in the sections that follow.

Description of God's wisdom

The apostle addresses praise to the only One who can truly be considered infinitely wise. He is appropriately ascribed as "the only wise God" (Rom. 16:27). It is with great awe and wonder that Paul not only considers God's knowledge but also His wisdom (Rom. 11:33). The context of Romans 11:33 notes that this wisdom is associated with God's sovereign plan of salvation as it relates to both Jew and Gentiles; and the apostle confesses that there is a certain incomprehensible nature to God's wisdom. However, it is clear that "God's work for man is seen to spring from his wisdom."[32] The wisdom of God has been defined as "the divine attribute according to which God arranges his purposes and his plans, chooses his means, and brings forth the results, all of which is done in absolute perfection."[33] It is the use of God's knowledge for its highest purpose as the most effective means are used for the attainment of the highest goals.[34] Wisdom is therefore the flower of knowledge and knowledge is the root of wisdom. As Guthrie has said, "Perfect wisdom presupposes perfect knowledge."[35]

God's wisdom is described as "manifold" and is connected with His eternal purpose (Eph. 3:10-11). Πολυποίκιλος is used only in Ephesians 3:10 in the New Testament. It literally means "multi-colored" or "much-variegated."[36] It calls attention to the infinite diversity and sparkling beauty of God's wisdom.[37] There is diversity and yet perfect harmony in all that is associated with God's wisdom. Lenski makes this point when he writes:

> God's wisdom is one, yet it can be termed "multifarious" because it weaves a thousand apparently tangled threads into one glorious pattern. So out of the most diverse elements, where the strongest opposites clashed, where men saw only impossibilities, God, coming with means which looked hopelessly inadequate to men, worked out results which no man would have dreamed, and no angel could have foreseen.[38]

The emphasis in Paul's treatment of the wisdom of God is on the means God chose to solve the "complicated problem of man's redemption," which is the "unsearchable riches of the work of Christ."[39] As Guthrie says, "This is regarded in NT thought as the supreme manifestation of wisdom."[40] In the wisdom of God or in "God's all-wise purpose,"[41] the means that God chose for salvation was faith in Christ's work, which excluded the possibility of His being known through human wisdom (1 Cor. 1:21). In this sense Christ is the wisdom of God, because in Him the divine plan of salvation is revealed and mediated to men (1 Cor. 1: 23-24).[42] Since in Christ all the treasures of wisdom and knowledge are hidden (Col. 2:3), "the wisdom of God is most manifestly operative in what Christ did and was."[43] In His wisdom God has arranged all His works so as to exclude all human boasting (Rom. 3:27, 4:2, 11:32; 1 Cor. 1:29). This governs wisdom's choice of all proper means. It is for this reason that the Pauline treatment of the wisdom of God has its emphasis on the work of Christ which is a means that excludes all human boasting and results in the praise of His glory (Eph. 1:12, 14). It is only God's wisdom that can author a plan that has as its goal and climax that "God may be all in all" (1 Cor. 15:28).

Contrasted with worldly wisdom

Full consideration of the meaning of the wisdom of God in Pauline theology must take into account what is said concerning its contrast with worldly wisdom. "Men have closed their minds to the wisdom of God" and have "attempted to create their own wisdom (1 Cor. 1:21; cf. Rom. 1:18ff.)."[44] The wisdom of the world is termed the "wisdom of this age" (1 Cor. 2:6), "human wisdom" (1 Cor. 2:13), and "fleshy wisdom" (2 Cor. 1:12). It is based on the rejection of God's revelation (Rom. 1:21-23) and is the author of "self-made religion" (Col. 2:23). It is viewed in contrast to the grace of God (2 Cor. 1:12) and the teaching ministry of the Spirit (1 Cor. 2:13). It is a wisdom of words in which there is a greater concern for how something is said than with what is being said (1 Cor. 1:17; 2:1, 4, 5, 13).[45] It is this that Paul avoided when he preached the gospel in the power of the Spirit. It is a wisdom that not only does not give proper attention to the cross of Christ (1 Cor. 1:17) but is in fact in opposition to the message of the cross (1 Cor. 1:21). It is a wisdom that is limited to the affairs of this age and has no knowledge of the things that really matter (1 Cor. 1:20, 26; 2:6; 3:18). It falls short of a knowledge of God as Paul writes that "the world through its wisdom did not come to know God" (1 Cor. 1:21). The depth of the error of worldly wisdom is seen in its evaluation of Christ who is the wisdom of God (1 Cor. 1:24). Worldly wisdom looks at Christ as foolishness (1 Cor. 1:18, 23; cf. 2:8) while God looks at the wisdom of the world and regards it as foolishness (1 Cor. 3:19). Human wisdom makes its boast in men (1 Cor. 3:4, 21) while God's wisdom chooses means and ends that shame the wise of the world (1 Cor. 1:27) and enable no man to boast before God (1 Cor. 1:29).

God's wisdom cannot be understood and appreciated until a proper evaluation of human wisdom is made. "Σοφία is obviously a catch-word of Paul's opponents."[46] The foolishness of God is wiser than men (1 Cor. 1:25) in that "the lowest manifestation of divine wisdom exceeds the highest results of the wisdom of men."[47] In fact God has judged human wisdom and Paul's quote of Isaiah 29:14 refers to this judgment (1 Cor. 1:19). Human wisdom will never be able to achieve a final exaltation over divine revelation. While the wisdom of the world regards the word of the cross as foolishness (1 Cor. 1:18), this false evaluation will not be permitted to triumph. Paul's quote of Job 5:13 also substantiates the fact of God's response to "worldly wisdom" (1 Cor. 3:19).

In addition to stating that human wisdom is inferior and will not triumph over God's wisdom, Paul underscores the basic difference between the two. "God's power and wisdom show themselves in a way which is not in accordance with men's 'a priori' standards: they altogether transcend such standards."[48] However, the comparison reaches its climax when the apostle declares worldly wisdom to be foolishness. He is not content to consider it as merely inferior and different, but it must be regarded as foolishness before God (1 Cor. 3:19). It is wisdom only by a false profession (Rom. 1:22). It is in the death of Christ that God has made foolish the wisdom of the world in that in it He achieved what human wisdom failed to achieve (1 Cor. 1:20-21). While it may deceive its victims (Rom. 1:22, 1 Cor. 3:18), the Lord's evaluation of it is that it is useless (1 Cor. 3:20). It is this wisdom that Paul did not employ in his ministry (1 Cor. 1:17; 2:1, 4) for he knew that it was an inappropriate resting place for men's faith (1 Cor. 2:5).

Display of God's wisdom in the church

As the believer stands in awe and wonder at God's wisdom which is seen in a striking contrast to the wisdom of the world, he is to become increasingly like God in letting His wisdom guide His life. As in the Old Testament wisdom is ascribed more to man as God's gift than to God as His attribute, although the latter is certainly true in both Testaments. However, additional insights into the development of Paul's teaching on this aspect of God's character can be seen in its display in the life of the church. The pathway to becoming wise is to first admit that one is foolish (1 Cor. 3:18; cf. Rom. 1:22) for wisdom is to be understood as a "gift of the grace of God . . . in which the believer may grow"[49] (Eph. 1:8, 17; Col. 1:9). It is an object of prayer (Eph. 1:17; Col. 1:9) and is to guide one's entire life (Eph. 5:15-16) and specifically his teaching others (Col. 1:28, 3:16), for "admonition, however well-intentioned it may be, can provoke the opposite result to that which is desired if it be given in an unwise or tactless manner."[50] Wisdom is also to guide the believer's dealings with unbelievers for "the reputation of the gospel is bound up with the conduct of those who claim to have experienced its saving power"[51] (Col. 4:5). Wisdom can be taught as Paul mentions speaking wisdom among mature Christians (1 Cor. 2:6-7).[52] It is vitally connected with the indwelling of the word of Christ, which is a prerequisite for the believers to fulfill their duty of teaching and admonishing one another (Col. 3:16), as well as with the Holy Spirit, for it is spiritual wisdom that is the concern of Paul's prayer (Col. 1:9). The Spirit and the Word aid one to discern the teachings that have only "an appearance of wisdom" (Col. 2:23).

Ephesians 5:15-17 is a key verse in regard to the display of God's wisdom in the church. Richardson maintains that "from this verse we may deduce the full biblical meaning og 'wise' and 'foolish.'"[53] The opposite of walking as an unwise man is walking as a wise man which is described by the phrase ἐξαγοραζόμενοι τον καιρόν, which occurs not only in Ephesians 5:16 but also in Colossians 4:5. The best translation is probably "make the most of the time."[54] The wise walk involves a careful watchfulness so as to pay the necessary price in time and effort in order to grasp every possible opportunity "for fulfilling Christian duty and displaying spiritual fruit."[55] The use of the phrase in Colossians 4:5 refers specifically to a believer's dealings with those outside the church while in Ephesians 5:16 it is a general reference that refers to the whole of the believer's life. 'Εξαγοράζω occurs in the middle voice in these verses which carries the idea of "buying up for yourself."[56] The price that is to be paid is the required pain and effort.[57] Καιρός has the meaning of not just time but opportunity, the fit time.[58] The believer is to realize that his time is limited and that his life presents only so many opportunities.

He is to invest his all in every one and realize that it may be a lack of wisdom "to hold back and wait for a still better opportunity."[59] The days are evil (Eph. 5:16) and as a result they pressure one to misuse his time, and it is the wise walk of the believer that reflects God's light in the darkness of the evil days. The other antithesis to being foolish is understanding the will of the Lord (Eph. 5:17). Συνίημι occurs in the imperative form and the command involves an intelligent comprehension of the will of the Lord and not just an acquaintance or mere matter of fact knowledge.[60] In order to be watchful, earnest, and zealous in making the most of the opportunities that present themselves, one cannot depend on his own acumen or the advice of others as the ultimate guide. He must understand the revealed will of God and let this be his standard and guide.[61]

Additional insight can be gained through the instruction given in Romans 16:19. In this verse one reads of the apostle's desire for the Roman church to be wise in what is good and innocent in what is evil. In regard to the first part of the exhortation, the believer is to be "practically wise in the pursuit of good."[62] The believer is to consider the time, manner, and means so that he does not "spoil a good thing by the unwise or unskillful way in which it is gone about."[63] The second part of the exhortation refers to the believer's relationship to evil. Ἀκέραιος is used to describe this relationship. Barclay comments on the meaning of this word:

> It is used of metal which has no suspicion of alloy, of wine and of milk which are pure and not adulterated with water. It describes something which is absolutely pure of any kind of taint or corruption.[64]

The believer's life is to be pure from any contamination of evil so that he may be as a babe in respect to evil (1 Cor. 14:20). This is possible only as he resolves to turn away from the falst teachers to whom he has previously referred (Rom. 16:17). The wisdom of God is displayed in the church that learns to detect evil from its knowledge of purity. There is much earthly wisdom that has an evil root, and the believer should turn away from it that he may not be tainted by it.

God's wisdom excludes human boasting while human wisdom promotes it. Therefore, the display of God's wisdom in the church is seen in the absence of self-glorification and party divisions. Therefore, Brown is correct when, in reference to God's wisdom, he states that "it is the foundation of the unity of the Chrisian church."[65]

The life of the church is to be characterized by σοφία, φρόνησις, and σύνεσις. Both φρόνησις and σύνεσις are special applications of σιφία. Berry defines σοφία in the following way:

> It denotes mental excellence in the highest and fullest sense, expressing an 'attitude' as well as an 'act' of the mind. It comprehends knowledge and implies goodness, including the striving after the highest ends, as well as the using of the best means for their attainment.[66]

Φρόνησις is "above all the ability to deal with a given situation; it is the ability to see what needs to be done and to do it; it is the practical wisdom of a man who is never at a loss."[67] Σύνεσις is the wise judgment that "can see the implication of a thing and the ultimate end of a course of action."[68] All of these are true of God in an infinite sense but are mediated to believers and are to be displayed in the life of the church.

Notes

[1]TNIDNTT, s.v. "γινώσκω," by E. D. Schmitz, 2 (1976): 397.

[2]Ibid., 2 (1976):400. [3]Ibid.

[4]Archibald Robinson and Alfred Plummer, A Critical and Exegetical Commentary on the First Epistle of St. Paul to the Corinthians, ICC, p. 299. Also related is Paul's use of προγινώσκω which will be discussed under the sovereignty of God.

[5]W. E. Vine, The Expository Dictionary of New Testament Words, 4 vols., 2:298.

[6]C. E. B. Cranfield, A Critical and Exegetical Commentary on the Epistle to the Romans, ICC, 2 vols., 2:589-90.

[7]Vine, 2:298.

[8]Donald W. Burdick, "Οἶδα and Γινώσκω in the Pauline Epistles," in New Dimensions in New Testament Study, eds. Richard N. Longenecker and Merrill C. Tenney, p. 354.

[9]Ibid. [10]Ibid.

[11]Charles Hodge, Commentary on the Epistle to the Romans, p. 378.

[12]John Murray, The Epistle to the Romans, NIC, 2 vols., 2:105-6.

[13]William G. T. Shedd, A Critical and Doctrinal Commentary on the Epistle of St. Paul to the Romans, p. 354.

[14]Ibid. [15]Murray, 2:106.

[16]Charles Hodge, An Exposition of the First Epistle to the Corinthians, p. 45.

[17]C. K. Barrett, The First Epistle to the Corinthians, HNTC, p. 78.

[18]R. C. H. Lenski, The Interpretation of St. Paul's First and Second Epistles to the Corinthians, p. 119.

[19]Edward J. Young, The Book of Isaiah, NIC, 3 vols., 3:45.

[20]Hodge, Romans, p. 279.

[21]TDNT, s.v. "γινώσκω," by Rudolph Bultmann, 1 (1964): 706.

[22]See Charles C. Ryrie, Biblical Theology of the New Testament, pp. 211-17.

[23]George Ricker Berry, A Dictionary of New Testament Greek Synonyms, pp. 19-20.

[24]H. C. G. Moule, Studies in Colossians and Philemon, KPC, p. 68.

[25]W. H. Griffith Thomas, Studies in Colossians and Philemon, p. 111.

[26]Moule, p. 125.

[27]John Eadie, Commentary on the Epistle of Paul to the Colossians, p. 230.

[28]Henry Liddell and George Scott, A Greek-English Lexicon, s.v. "σοφία," pp. 1621-22. In the sense of theoretical knowledge, the meaning of σοφία differed in the various philosophical schools. For a succinct summary of the use of σοφία in Greek philosophy see TNIDNTT, s.v. "σοφία," by J. Goetzmann, 3 (1978):1027.

[29]TDNT, s.v. "σοφία," by Ulrich Wilckens, 7 (1971): 496.

[30]Berry, p. 19.

[31]It is also associated with Christ in such passages as Matthew 13:54, Mark 6:2, Luke 2:40, and 2:52.

[32]Donald Guthrie, New Testament Theology, p. 95.

[33]R. C. H. Lenski, The Interpretation of St. Paul's Epistles to the Galatians, Ephesians, and Philippians, p. 482.

[34]William Hendriksen, New Testament Commentary--Exposition of Ephesians, p. 84.

[35]Guthrie, p. 95.

[36]Hendriksen, Ephesians, p. 159.

[37]Ibid. [38]Lenski, pp. 482-83.

[39]H. C. G. Moule, Studies in Epheisans, KPC, p. 92.

[40]Guthrie, p. 95.

[41]W. Harold Mare, Romans--Galatians, in EBC, 12 vols., 10:197.

[42]E. Earle Ellis, Prophecy and Hermeneutic in Early Christianity, p. 59.

[43]A Theological Word Book of the Bible, s.v. "Wise, wisdom," by E. C. Blackman, p. 283.

[44]TNIDNTT, s.v. "σοφία," by Colin Brown, 3 (1978): 1031.

[45]William Barclay, New Testament Words, p. 265.

[46]TDNT, s.v. "σοφία," by Ulrich Wilckens, 7 (1971): 523.

[47]Hodge, 1 Corinthians, p. 24.

[48]Archibald Robertson and Alfred Plummer, A Critical and Exegetical Commentary on the First Epistle of St. Paul to the Corinthians, ICC, p. 23.

[49]TNIDNTT, s.v. "σοφία," by Colin Brown, 3 (1978): 1032.

[50]E. K. Simpson and F. F. Bruce, Commentary on the Epistles to the Ephesians and the Colossians, NIC, p. 283.

[51]Ibid., p. 299. [52]Barclay, p. 264.

[53]A Theological Word Book of the Bible, s.v. "Folly, fool, foolish, foolishness," by Alan Richardson, p. 85.

[54]BAG, 4th rev. ed., s.v. "ἐξαγοράζω," p. 271.

[55]Homer A. Kent, Jr., Ephesians, EBC, p. 95.

[56]G. Abbott-Smith, A Manual Greek Lexicon of the New Testament, s.v. "εξαγοράζω," p. 158.

[57]T. K. Abbott, A Critical and Exegetical Commentary on the Epistles to the Ephesians and to the Colossians, ICC, p. 160.

[58]Richard C. Trench, Synonyms of the New Testament, pp. 209-12.

[59]Lenski, Galatians, Ephesians, and Philippians, p. 614.

[60]S. D. F. Salmond, in EGT, 5 vols., 3:362.

[61]Hendriksen, Ephesians, p. 238.

[62]H. P. Liddén, Explanatory Analysis of St. Paul's Epistle to the Romans, p. 302.

[63]F. L. Godet, Commentary on the Epistle to the Romans, p. 498.

[64]Barclay, p. 239.

[65]TNIDNTT, s.v. "σοφία," by Colin Brown, 3 (1978):1032.

[66]Berry, p. 19. [67]Barclay, p. 267. [68]Ibid.

CHAPTER III

MORAL ATTRIBUTES IN PAULINE THEOLOGY

The Love of God

In the New Testament, it is only the Apostle Paul that specifically uses the title "God of love" (2 Cor. 13: 11).[1] The attribute of love is mentioned in relation to each Person of the Trinity (Rom. 8:35, 15:30; 2 Cor. 13:14). Paul discussed God's love not in a theoretical or abstract way but writes from his personal experience for he was certain that "for him the Lord had climbed Calvary."[2] He wrote that the pursuit of the believer's life should be God's love (1 Cor. 14:1) for it is a vital ingredient into any Christian activity (1 Cor. 13:1-3). For this reason he affirmed the goal of his instruction to be love (1 Tim. 1:5), and his prayer for believers was that the Lord would direct their hearts into the love of God (2 Thess. 3:5). Sheldon refers to the love of God as "the primal motive power in the divine heart," and asserts that Paul's tribute to it is "limited only by the resources of his vocabulary."[3]

The lexical basis

Of the four Greek words for love, the verb ἀγαπάω and the corresponding noun ἀγάπη form the lexical basis for Paul's treatment of the love of God. Ἐράω and ἔρως are defined by Cranfield when he writes:

> [This root] denotes a love that is called forth by the inherent worth of its object, and desires to possess and enjoy its object. It is essentially egocentric, seeking its object for the sake of its own satisfaction and self-fulfillment and self-enhancement.[4]

It is mainly used for sexual love and never occurs in the New Testament.[5] Στοργέω and στοργή are used to denote family affection. While they may at times refer to the family relationship between a people and their ruler, they are more commonly used to describe the love between parents and children.[6] The verb is also rarely used of sexual love.[7] These words, likewise, do not occur in Paul's writings. The compound φιλόστοργος does occur in Romans 12:10 to denote the family affection within the Christian church. Likewise, the antonym ἄστοργος is used in Romans 1:31 and 2 Timothy 3:3. Φιλέω and φιλία were the most common words for love and primarily denote an affectionate regard for one's friend or marriage partner.[8] It may include physical love but is more inclusive and denotes a beautiful relationship that implies care and concern.[9] Unlike the Apostle John,[10] Paul never uses φιλέω to describe God's love for man. It is used once to describe man's love for Christ (1 Cor. 16:22) and once to describe love within the family of God (Titus 3:15). Φίλημα is used for the holy kiss (Rom. 16:16; 1 Cor. 16:20; 2 Cor. 13:12; 1 Thess. 5:26) and of the numerous compounds of φιλέω that occur in Paul, the most important in relationship to love as an attribute of God is φιλανθρωπία (Titus 3:4).

The revelation of God's love in Paul's writings is built around the use of ἀγαπάω and ἀγάπη. References to ἀγάπη in pre-biblical Greek are almost completely lacking.[11] While ἀγαπάω appears in Greek literature, its meaning is "weak and variable."[12] It is not always distinct from ἐράω and φιλέω. It is sometimes used of sexual love and can be interchanged with φιλέω.[13] When it is distinct from φιλέω, it lacks the warmth of the latter term.[14] However, ἀγαπάω has a distinctive nuance of "a giving, active love on the other's behalf" and indicates "more of a free and decisive act determined by its subject."[15] Significant is the fact that it may be used to denote "the preference of God for a particular man."[16] However, the meaning of ἀγαπάω is still imprecise.[17] In the LXX ἀγαπάω and ἀγάπη do emerge as the primary biblical words for love. They are primarily used to translate אהב and אהבה, which vary in their use and carry the connotations of all the Greek terms.[18] The translators' use of ἀγάπη as an opposite of μῖσος (Eccles. 9:1, 6) may have been out of a desire to choose a term that had the element of decisive choice.[19]

It is on the pages of the New Testament that the particular significance of ἀγαπάω and ἀγάπη is really discovered. The most pertinent issue for this study is, of course, how Paul uses these terms. His concept of the love of God cannot be understood apart from its unique demonstration in Christ's dying for the helpless, ungodly, sinful, and His enemies (Rom. 5:6-10). Therein lies the meaning of ἀγαπάω and ἀγάπη. While the historical event is recorded in the Gospels, in Paul's Epistles one finds the chief interpretation of it.

One might ask, "Why did the New Testament writers and in particular the Apostle Paul choose ἀγαπάω instead of the other Greek words for love?" God's love, which is described in the following sections, is certainly not limited to sexual passion as ἐράω would indicate. Likewise, στοργέω and φιλέω are too exclusive, for God's love goes beyond a love that is based on the attractiveness and desirableness of the object loved such as one's family or friends; and it even extends to one's enemies. Ἀγαπάω and ἀγάπη were the only words "capable of being filled with the content which was required."[20] As Cranfield points out, "The root was presumably chosen, because it was free from erotic associations and conveyed the idea of a love that showed itself by helping its object rather than by desiring to possess and enjoy it, and also because of its very indistinctness of range fitted it to receive the OT associations of <u>aheb</u>."[21] Therefore, it can be said that the New Testament writers and most important for this study the Apostle Paul "take up a rather colourless word and indefinitely enrich it."[22] In the New Testament it can be said that ἀγαπάω has been "purged of all coldness and is deeper than φιλεῖν, though the latter remains more human."[23] Vine remarks that, in respect to God, ἀγαπάω "expresses the deep and constant love and interest of a perfect Being toward entirely unworthy objects, producing a reverential love in them toward the Giver, and a practical love toward those who are partakers of the same, and a desire to help others to seek the Giver."[24]

Display of God's love

While love is an eternal attribute of God, it was uniquely displayed at a point in history. This point of history, of course, centers around the historical appearing and death of Jesus Christ. As Cranfield has said, "All that the NT and for that matter the OT too, has to say about the love of God to man is expressed in the two words, 'Jesus Christ.'"[25] The classic text in Paul's writings is Romans 5:6-8, which Cremer considers as even more profound than any of John's writings, the apostle of love.[26] It is significant that in Romans 5:8 συνίστημι is in the present tense, while the aorist (ἀπέθανεν) describes the past event of the cross. This past event is a continual demonstration[27] of God's love. The act of Christ's death, which in Romans 5:8 is referred to by the aorist of ἀποθνήσκω, is characteristically referred to by the aorist of ἀγαπάω in Paul (Rom. 8:37; Gal. 2:20; Eph. 2:4, 5:2, 25; 2 Thess. 2:16). "In the coming of Christ and the consequent proclamation of the Gospel,"[28] Paul declares that the love of God has appeared in that it has "come to public view"[29] (Titus 3:4).

Objects of God's love

Christ. One of the titles of Christ is "the Beloved." Ἐν τῷ ἠγαπημένῳ occurs only in Ephesians 1:6; but the corresponding phrase, τοῦ υἱου τῆς ἀγάπης αὐτοῦ, is in Colossians 1:13. God is a "God of love" (2 Cor. 13:11) and this attribute of love is not only mentioned with each Person of the Trinity (Rom. 8:35, 15:30; 2 Cor. 13:14), but it is shared among the Persons of the Trinity as these two descriptions of Christ imply (Eph. 1:6; Col. 1:13). The Son is "the blessed object of the Father's love."[30]

All men. God's love for all men is seen in Romans 5:6-8. Romans 1:18--3:20 provides the background to assure one that the terms "helpless," "ungodly," and "sinners" are a fitting description of all and not just a part of the human race. The fact that it is the Lord who enables the believer to love not only other believers but all men also testifies to the truth of God's universal love (1 Thess. 3:12). God is not pleased with man's sin and "the wrath of God has to do with the sinner in the man," but His love applies to the "man in the sinner."[31] As Moffatt says, "The range of the divine love is universal; God is willing to be the Father of all and any, no matter what their national or earlier heritage may have been; a Jewish birth does not qualify by itself, so neither does pagan birth disqualify; the love of God is open to the human race."[32]

<u>Believers</u>. Believers are referred to as the "beloved of God" (Rom. 1:7). Since Paul is an imitator of God (Eph. 5:1), he also refers to believers as his beloved (Rom. 16:8) and exhorts all believers to walk in love (Rom. 13:8; Eph. 5:2). However, the present focus is on the fact that believers are special objects of God's love. In classical Greek ἀγαπητός is used of a child and "particularly of an only child to whom all the love of his parents is given."[33] On rare occasions it could refer to "someone favoured by a God."[34] The perfect passive participle ἠγαπημένοι occurs in 1 Thessalonians 1:4, 2 Thessalonians 2:13, and Colossians 3:12 to denote a love "which existed in the past but continues into the present with unabated force."[35] God has set His love upon all of His children, and because He is infinite He can love each one as if they were the only one He had to care for (cf. John 17:23; Gal. 2:20). Since all three of the verses (1 Thess. 1:4; 2 Thess. 2:13; Col. 3:12) explicitly contain the idea of God's election,[36] one infers that God has set His love upon them at the time of His choosing them. Therefore, while the world has a present demonstration of God's love, in that the past event of the cross is a continual revelation of it (Rom. 5:8), the believer lives in the perpetual experience of this love (Rom. 8:38-39). Therefore, the apostle writes of the love of God "which is in Christ Jesus our Lord" (Rom. 8:39) not only because in Christ Jesus is God's love supremely displayed; but also because the

believer has by God's electing love been chosen in Christ (Eph. 1:4) and by virtue of being "in Christ" lives in the sphere of the love of God, which has been poured out within his heart through the Holy Spirit (Rom. 5:5). The cross is the reminder that God has a persistent desire to further the welfare of His children who are unique objects of His love (Rom. 8:32).

Israel. In Romans 11:28 Israel is termed the beloved of God. Murray defines the phrase when he writes, "'Beloved' thus means that God has not suspended or rescinded his relation to Israel as his chosen people in terms of the covenants made with the fathers."[37]

Righteousness. In 2 Corinthians 9:7 Paul writes that God loves a cheerful giver, which may be an allusion to Proverbs 22:9. The verse teaches that God loves a heart that gives not grudgingly but cheerfully. This is the kind of heart that is in conformity with the heart of God (cf. 2 Cor. 8:9). God loves that which conforms to His righteous standards. In that vein 2 Corinthians 9:7 is a particular application of the general principle of Psalm 11:7 that God is righteous and loves righteousness. Paul even refers to a special manifested presence of the God of love to the obedient believer (2 Cor. 13:11; cf. John 14:21, 23).

Description of God's love

Sacrificial. It has already been noted that the

supreme display of God's love was in the death of Christ (Rom. 5:8). This involved the giving up of Oneself for the temporal and eternal benefit of another. This is expressed by the παραδόντος ἑαυτὸν ὑπερ ἐμοῦ of Galatians 2:20, the παρέδωκεν ἑαυτὸν ὑπερ ἡμων of Ephesians 5:2, and the ἑαυτὸν παρέδωκεν ὑπερ αὐτῆς of Ephesians 5:25. As this love was produced in Paul's life by the Spirit (Gal. 5:22), one sees his willingness to sacrifice himself for the benefit of others (Rom. 9:3; 1 Thess. 2:8). This self sacrifice, which Moffatt terms "the highest form of love known to us,"[38] is the opposite of being consumed with one's own interests (1 Cor. 13:5; cf. Phil. 2:21). It involves the sincere desire (Rom. 12:9; 2 Cor. 6:6, 8:8) to benefit and not harm others (cf. Rom. 14:15).

Paul's conception of God's attitude to man is clearly revealed in his descriptions of God's love. As Kennedy puts it, "God's disposition towards them is not cold, not even impartial. He yearns for man's love. Christ's sacrifice, which is God's sacrifice, is the convincing demonstration of it."[39] Bound up in the very Being of God is the disposition to freely give of Himself at the expense of great suffering to benefit others (Rom. 8:32). It is a quality that has been supremely expressed in Christ (2 Cor. 8:9, cf. 8:24), who both personifies and mediates God's love. The death of Christ exposes the heart of God as a heart of love. God exists not only to be loved but also to love.

Universal. God's love is a love that extends to all men. The supreme demonstration of this fact is the provision of a Saviour for all men (Rom. 5:6-8; 1 Tim. 4:10).

Personal. The personalization of God's love is most clearly seen in Galatians 2:20, where the apostle personalizes God's love in relation to himself.

Electing. The love of God in Paul's writings is an electing love.[40] This is seen throughout Paul's writings (cf. Col. 3:12; 1 Thess. 1:4; 2 Thess. 2:13) and has already been referred to in noting the objects of God's love.[41] God's love prompted Him not only to send His Son to die but also to set His love upon those He chooses out of a world which is in rebellion against Him and deserves His wrath. The recipients of His electing love are to respond by exemplifying His love to others (Col. 3:12-14).

Righteous. The love of God is a righteous love as the same historical event that demonstrated His love (Rom. 5:8) also demonstrated His righteousness (Rom. 3:25). Christ's giving up of Himself was a service and sacrifice to God (Eph. 5:2) in which sin was judged as the beloved Son bore the judgment Himself (Rom. 8:3; 2 Cor. 5:21). The love of God will not violate the righteousness of God which guides the believer into the knowledge of how to truly benefit another (Rom. 13:8-10; Gal. 5:14). The love of God is a righteous love which does not act unbecomingly and cannot rejoice with unrighteousness (1 Cor. 13:5-6). While the reader of Paul's revelation might not understand all the reasons behind the sovereign display of God's love, the answer does not lie in any injustice with God whose love is righteous (cf. Rom. 9:15).

Wise. God's love is also viewed as being in accordance with His wisdom. The supreme demonstration of God's love was at the perfect time (Rom. 5:6; Gal. 4:4). Likewise, all of God's actions which are motivated by His love result in praise to God (Eph. 1:6, 12, 14).[42] While knowledge and insight are to guide the believer's love (Phil. 1:9-10), God's love is guided by His omniscience and wisdom.

Unmerited. Vine alludes to the unmerited nature of God's love when he writes, "It was an exercise of the Divine will in deliberate choice, made without assignable cause save that which lies in the nature of God Himself."[43] Vine is referring to the death of Christ which was in behalf of the helpless, ungodly, sinners, and His enemies (Rom. 5:6-10). It is in this sense that the love of God differs from the love of man. The apostle challenges the readers to think of the most noble and loving person he knows and assures them that this love falls far short of God's love (Rom. 5:7). God's love is directed at those who do not deserve it (Eph. 2:1-3), because it is a merciful love (Eph. 2:4).

Conquering. It is a conquering love in the sense that the God of love has won the believer by His loving call and this love has a controlling influence on the believer's life (2 Cor. 5:14). In 2 Corinthians 5:14 συνέχει has the force of confining one in the sense of being between two walls. The love is defined in 2 Corinthians 5:14-15 as the death of Christ and the confinement as a life that is lived for Christ and not for oneself.[44] However, God's love not only conquers the believer but also enables him to be a conqueror (Rom. 8:37). It "defies all the powers of heaven and earth"[45] in that it is stronger than any force that attempts to separate the believer from the love of God (Rom. 8:38-39).

Continual. It is a love that has been displayed as Paul always speaks of the death of Christ in the aorist. However, the continual nature of God's love is clearly seen in the perfect passive participle of ἀγαπάω (Col. 3:12; 1 Thess 1:4; 2 Thess. 2:13), the perfect passive indicative of ἐκχέω (Rom. 5:5), and the forceful argument of Romans 8:35-39. The very formula "in Christ" "speaks of existence of the believer in the love of God."[46] God's love is said to never fail (1 Cor. 13:8) and Paul affirms that it will continually abide (1 Cor. 13:13).

Surpasses knowledge. Various adjectives have been chosen to describe the love of God in Paul's writings. These adjectives have been chosen as those which naturally appeared from an inductive study of the Epistles. All the attributes that are yet to be discussed certainly in some sense help to describe God's love. However, no list of adjectives can give a complete description of God's love, as God's love surpasses knowledge as noted by the τὴν ὑπερβάλλουσαν τῆς γνώσεως of Ephesians 3:19. The reader of Paul's letter to the Ephesians has already encountered a power that surpasses greatness (Eph. 1:19) and a grace that surpasses riches (Eph. 2:7), which has prepared him for this love that surpasses knowledge. The prayer of Ephesians 3:14-19 appears to be avoiding two extremes. On the one hand, the love of Christ can be comprehended as evidenced by καταλαβέσθαι in 3:18. This comprehension or perception is dependent upon a right relationship with the Holy Spirit (Eph. 3:16-17) and with the body of Christ, the latter being inferred from the σύν πᾶσιν τοῖς ἁγίοις of Ephesians 3:18.[47] On the other hand, one should so comprehend the full dimensions[48] of Christ's love that he will never sense that his comprehension is exhaustive or complete.[49] It is progressively comprehended as it is progressively experienced.[50] As Hendriksen has stated:

> This love is so great that it defies all definition. We can speak of it as his intense concern for, deep personal interest in, warm attachment to, and spontaneous tenderness toward his chosen ones, but all this is but to stammer. Those, and those only, who experience it are the ones who know what it is, though even they can never fully comprehend it (3:19).[51]

The Mercy of God

The God of the Apostle Paul is the Father of mercies (2 Cor. 1:3). He testifies to the fact that to this mercy He owes his own salvation (1 Tim. 1:16) and declares that "there is an inexhaustible treasure of mercy in the loving heart of God."[52] The mercy of God is seen as a key motivation for a dedicated life for as Murray states, "It is the mercy of God that melts the heart and it is as we are moved by these mercies of God that we shall know the constraint of consecration as it pertains to our body (cf. 1 Cor. 6:20)."[53] Likewise, the experience of it according to Paul should compel the believer to glorify God for His mercy (Rom. 15:9; 2 Cor. 1:3). It is a key attribute in Paul's writings. As Guthrie says:

> There is no suggestion that the quality of mercy is alien to God, nor that it conflicts with his essential righteousness. It is part of the apostle's understanding of the total nature of God.[54]

The lexical basis

The revelation of the mercy of God in Paul's writings revolves around the use of ἔλεος, ἐλεέω, οἰκτιρμός, and οἰκτίρω. In classical Greek ἔλεος referred to "the emotion roused by contact with an affliction which comes undeservedly on someone else."[55] The verb ἐλεέω meant "to have compassion, be sorry for, show compassion, be merciful."[56] The cry ἐλέησον was addressed to the gods, a use that the Gospels approximate when they record the cry of the needy to Jesus

(Matt. 9:27, 15:22, 17:15, 20:30-31, Mark 10:47-48; Luke 18:38-39). In fact ἔλεος itself was even personified and worshiped.[58] Ἔλεος normally represents חסד in the LXX and less frequently רחמים. From the point of view that חסד in relationship to God denoted "His faithful and merciful help," it "is expressed in the use of ἔλεος."[59] The ἔλεος was thought of as a gracious gift because of Yahweh's superiority as the partner in the covenant.[60] While רחמים, which was often linked with חסד, carried more of an emotional content; it denoted not just the emotion but the act and expression of the compassion and love.[61] Ἐλεεω is primarily used for חנן and the Piel of רחם.[60] Both of these Hebrew words denote "gracious actions rather than just emotion."[63] The focus of חנן is on the graciousness of an action of a superior to an inferior. רחם in the Piel is used for a deep inward feeling which found expression in God's granting of forgiveness (Deut. 13:17) and which will find expression in the fulfillment of eschatological hope of Israel (Isa. 14:1). Οἰκτιρμός is used for the emotion of sympathy and οἰκτίρω meant to be sympathetic with a sympathy which was ready to help.[64] In the LXX οἰκτίρω is used almost always for חנן and רחם.[65] Οἰκτιρμός occurs almost exclusively for רחמים.[66] It is used with very little distinction from ἔλεος.[67] While the Greek idea of compassion and sympathetic help as well as the ideas of חסד, רחם, and חנן have prepared the reader of Paul's Epistles for his treatment of the mercy of God, it is only what God has done in Christ that can adequately express it (Titus 3:5-7). In Christ one sees the supreme expression of God's חסד, the supreme gift of חנן, and the deep feelings of רחם. The Gospels record the cry of the needy to Jesus to show mercy, the idea that the coming of Christ was merciful in that it was an act of God's faithfulness to His covenant (Luke 1:54-55, 72, 78), merciful gifts to individuals such as a child to the barren Elizabeth (Luke 1:58), and the many merciful acts and teachings of Jesus which illustrated mercy (cf. Matt. 18:21-35; Luke 10:25-37). However, it is the duty of the Apostle Paul to write of the mercy of God from the vantage point of the other side of the cross. The following sections are an attempt to display his treatment of this attribute.

The need of God's mercy

The universal need for God's mercy is not only clearly spelled out in Paul's cogent argument in Romans 1:18--3:20 but also in the single verse of Romans 11:32. In this verse all men, whether they be Jew or Gentile, are pictured as "imprisoned in their disobedience in such a way that they have no possibility of escape except as God's mercy releases them."[68]

The display of God's mercy

God is one who is filled with sympathy toward the miserable, afflicted, and distressed. This sympathy is joined by an active desire to relieve them. As Vine says, ἔλεος is the "outward manifestation of pity."[69]

In the salvation of men. It is the God who is rich in mercy who has not only withheld judgment but also raised the spiritual dead and seated them with Christ in heavenly places (Eph. 2:4-6). According to Moule, "The ultimate motive of the work of regeneration is here given, and it is simply the Divine mercy."[70] He continues on this point when he states, "No claim or obligation is in the question, nor right inherent in the alienated race, nor 'fitness of things' in the abstract; only the uncaused and supremely free choice of the God of mercy."[71] It is God's compassion for the helpless that motivates His action for their relief. Titus 3:5, likewise, notes that the basis of salvation is in accord with God's mercy, which is placed in sharp antithesis to the basis of man's righteous deeds.

In the appointment of men to the ministry. While Paul referred to his appointment to the ministry as a manifestation of God's grace (Gal. 2:9; Eph. 3:8), he also referred to it as an expression of God's mercy to him (1 Tim. 1:12-17). Paul sensed that his God had looked down and saw one who was living a wasteful and destructive life and in mercy granted him not only salvation but also the privilege of serving his Lord. This privilege was not only for Paul but included others as well (2 Cor. 4:1).

In the dispensing of aid to His ministers. Paul realized that God's mercy was not only involved in his appointment to the ministry, but he also could depend on it to sustain him in the ministry. In 2 Corinthians 4:1 Paul credits the mercy of God for his not losing heart in the midst of severe opposition and intense conflict. In like manner, it is the mercy of God that Paul credits for his being a trustworthy servant (1 Cor. 7:25). In commenting on 1 Corinthians 7:25 Hodge expresses this point when he writes, "Paul felt indebted to God for those inward qualities which entitled him to the confidence of his readers."[72]

It is for this reason that Paul's Epistles to Timothy contain his prayer that Timothy also might experience this mercy that equips and sustains one in the ministry (1 Tim. 1:2; 2 Tim. 1:2). Paul's love for his child in the faith led him to pray to God that He might give compassionate help to Timothy, whose situation and disposition His heavenly Father infinitely understood and felt. In this same manner, Paul's prayer for the house of Onesiphorus can be understood (2 Tim. 1:16). As Onesiphorus had shown mercy to Paul, the latter in turn prays to God to grant him mercy.[73] Paul's prayer for Timothy and Onesiphorus is also an appropriate prayer for all believers (Gal. 6:16) as Paul taught that all believers are to do the work of the ministry (Eph. 4:12). While every believer has already experienced God's mercy and are even termed vessels of mercy (Rom. 9:23), they are in need of an ever continuing supply of God's merciful help in their respective duties and difficulties (cf. Heb. 4:16). God is a Father of mercies to all His children (2 Cor. 1:3).

In the healing of the sick. God's mercy is said to have been displayed in the healing of Epaphroditus, who was sick to the point of death (Phil. 2:27). The object of mercy is stated to be not only Epaphroditus but also Paul, who would have been overburdened with sorrow if Epaphroditus would have died. Paul declares that God's heart is filled with mercy that expresses itself both to the sick and to those who are concerned for them. Does the Apostle teach that God always displays His mercy in this manner toward the sick? God is always a God of mercy to the sick but ultimate healing is not guaranteed to a believer until his body is redeemed (Rom. 8:23; cf. 2 Cor. 12:7-10; 2 Tim. 4:20).

In the comforting of the afflicted. It is in the various afflictions that the believer finds himself that he comes to know his God as the "Father of mercies" and "God of all comfort" (2 Cor. 1:3).[74] The phrase "Father of mercies" recalls the LXX use of οἰκτιρμός in Psalm 102 (103):13. It is not only true that "no suffering, however severe, can separate the believer from the tender care and compassion of his Heavenly Father,"[75] but that his afflictions are an opportunity to draw him closer to the Father of mercies. From the corresponding title--θεὸς πάσης παρακλήσεως--the πάσης declares

God to be the ultimate source of all comfort. The παρα-κλήσεως pictures God as the one who comes alongside of the afflicted to comfort and encourage them.[76] The comfort that is given will never fall short of what is needed (2 Cor. 1:5). As Hughes writes, "No matter how great the suffering a Christian is called upon to endure, they are matched and more than matched (cf. 4:17), by the comfort which God bestows."[77] He states it again by noting, "The comfort is never outweighed by the suffering."[78] In fact the comfort of the God of mercy is such that it meets the need of the afflicted and enables him to comfort others (2 Cor. 1:4).

<u>In the sanctification of the believer</u>. It is the mercies of God that are the basis for the Apostle's appeal to the believer to dedicate himself to God (Rom. 12:1-2). In this verse οἰκτιρμῶν refers to "the compassion of God revealed in God's dealing with man through Jesus Christ."[79] It is the mercy of God that furnishes the believer a proper motivation for a response of dedication to God. As Calvin has said, "Paul's entreaty teaches us that men will never worship God with a sincere heart, or be roused to fear and obey Him with sufficient zeal, until they properly understand how much they are indebted to His mercy."[80] Calvin also adds that Paul "reproaches us with ingratitude if, having had experience of so kind and liberal a father, we do not in return strive to dedicate ourselves wholly to Him."[81]

The mercy of God not only provides an adequate

motivation in regard to the believer's sanctification, but it is also seen as the basis of the continual renewing work of the Holy Spirit (Titus 3:5). The mercy of God is seen as God's motive in regenerating the believer, but the latter phrase in Titus 3:5--"renewing by the Holy Spirit"--appears to go beyond the previous phrase "washing of regeneration" and refers to the continual renewing work of the Holy Spirit.[82] While Romans 12:2 pictures this continual renewing from the human side, Titus 3:5 views it from the divine side as a merciful act of God.

In the distribution of rewards. This concept is seen in Paul's prayer that the Lord would grant Onesiphorus mercy when he stands in the presence of the Lord and his life is evaluated (2 Tim. 1:18).[83] Since the context (2 Tim. 1:16-18) is referring to the services that he rendered to Paul, the prayer is that God would remember him for these services. In Paul's letter to Timothy he is writing out his thoughts in God's presence and recalls this faithful one in the time that many others had deserted him. He is eager that this dear brother be rewarded, which is viewed in this passage as an expression of God's mercy.[84]

The description of God's mercy

Sufficient. The sufficiency of God's mercy is brought out by the πλούσιος ὢν ἐν ἐλέει of Ephesians 2:4.[85] The instruction that the gift of mercy is to be displayed with cheerfulness is also in keeping with the fact that one does not have to be stingy with this divine commodity (Rom. 12:8). Vine speaks of the sufficient nature of God's mercy when he notes that ἔλεος "assumes need on the part of him who receives it and resources adequate to meet that need on the part of him who shows it."[86]

Unmerited. The disobedience of man is the background for the display of God's mercy as indicated by the four references of ἀπειθεία in Romans 11:30-32. The disobedient human race is also described by Paul in Romans 3:10-18 and Ephesians 2:1-3. No one can say that on the basis of their own merit they have a claim on divine mercy. As Wood puts it, "Had he decided to destroy his refractory children, he would have been entirely justified, and nothing could have averted the catastrophe (Hos. 13:9)."[87] Paul is quite explicit about his own lack of merit when he states that he was a blasphemer, a persecutor, a violent aggressor, and the foremost of sinners (1 Tim. 1:13-15).

Sovereign. In God's display of mercy to the spiritual dead, enslaved, and condemned human race (Eph. 2:1-3), He is guided by His infinite wisdom and not by the merits of man. As Shedd has stated, "Mercy or compassion is a necessary feeling in the divine nature; but its manifestation toward persons is optional and sovereign."[88] The emphasis in Paul is on the freedom of God in displaying His overflowing mercy and compassion. It is this mercy that motivates God to make alive the spiritual dead, liberate the enslaved, and justify the condemned. The "mercy and compassion shown by God are determined by nothing external to His attributes."[89] The believer is to exemplify this compassion that God has shown him (Col. 3:12) and glorify God for His mercy (Rom. 15:9).

The Grace of God

Paul begins and ends his Epistles with a tribute to God's grace. From the time that he had encountered the risen Christ on the Damascus road, he had in Moffatt's words, sensed that "all is of grace, and grace is for all."[90] The work of salvation was to be an eternal exhibition of God's grace (Eph. 2:7). However, God's grace was also a part of the daily experience of Paul (1 Cor. 15:10). It was not only the basis for his ministry but also it was his message (Acts 20:24), which he guarded with great care (Gal. 2:21).

The lexical basis

The primary word for grace in Paul and the New Testament is χάρις. In the Greek language χάρις was a common word and its uses are well summarized by Robinson:

> (1) It was used objectively of that which causes a favorable regard or attractiveness; especially grace of form, gracefulness, and grace of speech, graciousness.
> (2) It was used subjectively of the favorable regard felt toward a person.
> (3) It was used of a definite favor.
> (4) It was used of the reciprocal feeling produced by a favor granted; that is, in the sense of gratitude.

(5) It was also used adverbially in phrases like "for the sake of a thing," charin tinos.[91]

In the LXX χάρις most frequently represents חן which has the connotation of "the stronger coming to the help of the weaker who stands in need of help by reason of his circumstances or natural weaknesses."[92] When it denotes the activity of God, it can stand for His election (Gen. 6:8) and His care for His covenant people (Exod. 33:12-16). Only twice is χάρις used for חסד and in these two cases it is virtually parallel to חן.[93]

While this background is helpful to keep in mind, χάρις had to be "virtually born again and baptized into Christ's spirit to express all that the NT sought to convey by it."[94] In expressing the message of Christ χάρις became "filled with a new and enriched content."[95] Trench makes the same observation when he states:

> There has often been occasions to observe the manner in which Greek words taken up into Christian use are glorified and transformed, seeming to have waited for this adoption of them, to come to their full rights, and to reveal all the depths and the riches of meaning which they contained, or might be made to contain. Χάρις is one of these.[96]

This is not to say that the earlier Greek uses of χάρις cannot be detected in the New Testament; however, "not all of them together convey the richness which the term acquired in the theology of Paul."[97] Of the 155 uses of χάρις in the New Testament, 100 of these are Paul's writings.[98]

Grace and the nature of God

Is the grace of God an action or an attribute of God? It appears to be both. It is an attribute that both has been expressed and does express itself in a variety of ways. Guthrie makes this observation when he notes, "God's grace is more than his gracious acts, although it includes these."[99] This same writer also observes, "This does not mean that grace is a static quality in God. It is rather the quality that prompts the acts of God."[100] Paul does not think of the attributes of God merely in the abstract. God is a God of love (2 Cor. 13:11) and He has demonstrated His love (Rom. 5:8). God is a God of mercy and He has expressed this mercy (1 Tim. 1:13). So it is with the grace of God. "God is gracious to us because he is gracious in himself first of all."[101] It is an attribute or characteristic of God and as Guthrie has stated, "If there was one characteristic of God which captured the imagination of Paul more than another, it was the grace of God."[102]

Display of the grace of God

In sending of His Son. It was in the historic occasion of God taking the form of a bondservant (Phil. 2:7) that the grace of God is said to have appeared (Titus 2:11). This appearing is a specific reference to the incarnation but would also "include his life, death, and resurrection."[103] It is in Christ's coming to earth that God's grace "'became visible,' 'came to light,' 'became clearly known.'"[104] God's grace came into clear view as the sun does at sunrise when Christ appeared in order to shine on those who were in darkness.[105] As the grace of the Triune God was manifested in Christ and mediated through Christ, it is also spoken of as the "grace of Christ" (Rom. 16:20; 1 Cor. 16:23; 2 Cor. 8:9, 13:14; Gal. 1:6, 6:18; Phil. 4:23; 1 Thess. 5:28; 2 Thess. 3:18; Philem. 25). The "appeared" of Titus 2:11 can be identified with "though He was rich, yet for your sake He became poor" (2 Cor. 8:9). The grace of God that was displayed in Christ's coming is the central message of Paul (Acts 14:3, 20:24, 32; 2 Cor. 4:15, 6:1; Gal. 2:21). While χάρις was used in Greek to denote a favor from the gods,[106] "before Bethlehem the concept of a God of grace who gives Himself appears nowhere."[107]

<u>In the appointment of Paul's ministry</u>. The apostle not only speaks of the grace of God as being manifested as an event in history (Titus 2:11) but also an event in his personal history (1 Tim. 1:14). Paul termed his very ministry as an apostle to the Gentiles as a special manifestation of God's grace (Rom. 15:15; 1 Cor. 3:10; Gal. 2:9; Eph. 3:7-8; Phil. 1:7). Even the revelation which God gave him is described by the verb χαρίζομαι (1 Cor. 2:12). He had no doubt that his ministry was a result of the grace of God.

<u>In electing</u>. God's election is based on His grace according to Romans 11:5-6. It is for that reason that God's

work of election (Eph 1:4) results in the praise of the glory of His grace (Eph. 1:6).

<u>In calling</u>. The historical outworking of God's election is in God's calling men into fellowship with His Son (1 Cor. 1:9). Paul testified to this fact in his own experience (Gal. 1:15) and reminded Timothy that God's call is due to His grace (2 Tim. 1:9).

<u>In justification</u>. The basis of God's justifying the ungodly is not their merit (Rom. 4:4-5; Eph. 2:9) but rather the grace of God (Rom. 3:24, 5:15, 17; Eph. 2:8; Titus 3:7). While the term "justify" is not used in 1 Thessalonians 2:16, this verse asserts that grace is the basis of God's giving "eternal comfort and good hope." Directly related is Paul's use of χάρισμα to refer to the gift of righteousness (Rom. 5:15-16) as well as the gift of eternal life (Rom. 6:23). The verb χαρίζομαι is used three times to speak of God's forgiveness (Eph. 4:32; Col. 2:13, 3:13). To underscore the gracious nature of God's act of justification, δωρέαν is used in Romans 3:24. It is the accusative of δωρεά and is used as an adverb. Of the nine other times it occurs in the New Testament, the most striking is in John 15:25 which asserts that they hated Christ "without a cause." In like manner, God has out of His grace justified the sinner without finding any cause to do so besides His own gracious nature. Likewise, δωρέαν underscores the fact that justification cannot be

purchased by man as suggested by its use in 2 Thessalonians 3:8, Revelation 21:6, and 22:17. It is this grace that Paul speaks of in recalling his own salvation (1 Tim. 1:14).

<u>In providing a new environment for the believer</u>. This is unquestionably related to God's act of justification but is broader in that it refers to the "state of justification."[108] It refers to God's providing the believer with a standing in grace (Rom. 5:2). The believer's feet have been firmly planted in the grace of God so as to enjoy the permanent state of being the objects of His favor. This new environment is also portrayed by grace being personified as a ruling king and the believer being a subject under its rule (Rom. 5:21, 6:14). It is for this reason that Paul says he conducted his life in the grace of God as opposed to fleshy wisdom which the Greek prided himself as his point of reference or environment (2 Cor. 1:12). This new environment is the believer's position in the Beloved where God has freely bestowed on him His favor (Eph. 1:6).[109] This new environment is attributed to the grace of God and is seen as the foundation for the believer's sanctification. To live under the reign of grace is to be liberated from the reign of sin (Rom. 5:21), which has been possible because of the believer's baptism into Christ (Rom. 6:1-10). Likewise, to live under grace (Rom. 6:14) is to be enslaved to obedience (Rom. 6:16), righteousness (Rom. 6:18), and God which results in sanctification (Rom. 6:22). In view of the connection between this

"state of justification" and sanctification, Paul views seeking to be justified by law as falling from grace (Gal. 5:4).[110] It is for this reason that Paul urged his converts to "continue in the grace of God" (Acts 13:43).

In the continual giving of aid to believers. All of Paul's Epistles contain a salutation and a benediction with a reference to grace. The conventional Greek opening of χαίρειν was replaced by Paul's χάρις and εἰρήνη (Rom. 1:7; 1 Cor. 1:3; 2 Cor. 1:2; Gal. 1:3; Eph. 1:2; Phil. 1:2; Col. 1:2; 1 Thess. 1:1; 2 Thess. 1:2; 1 Tim. 1:2; 2 Tim. 1:2; Titus 1:4; Philem. 3). The use of χάρις in the salutation denotes Paul's prayer[111] that God would graciously grant to them all the "rich abundance of his undeserved gifts."[112] It is therefore a reference to God's stored up help that He dispenses to His people in need (cf. Heb. 4:16). The conventional closing of ἔρρωσθε was replaced by χάρις. Moffatt comments, "That Paul struck out with a fresh conclusion to the Christian letter was more than a stylistic idiosyncracy; it indicates the dominant place of 'grace' in his religious vocabulary, and also the fact that this was recognized by his churches as characteristic of his own message."[113] While these benedictions differ slightly, they all contain a reference to χάρις (Rom. 16:20; 1 Cor. 16:23; 2 Cor. 13:14; Gal. 6:18; Eph. 6:24; Col. 4:18; 1 Thess. 5:28; 2 Thess. 3:18; 1 Tim. 6:21; 2 Tim. 4:22; Philem. 25). In all cases except in Ephesians, this grace is explicitly associated with Christ who both demonstrated and mediated God's grace. The benediction is a prayer that the grace of Christ would be with the believer, and in Galatians, Philippians, and Philemon μετὰ τοῦ πνεύματος ὑμῶν is used instead of μεθ' ὑμῶν. Burton notes that the benediction is a prayer that the believer "may have the indwelling gracious presence of the Lord Jesus Christ."[114] It could perhaps better be stated as a prayer that the believers would enjoy the dynamic working of the indwelling Christ, for the fact of Christ's indwelling presence is already clearly established (Rom. 8:9; Gal. 2:20). Paul's use of μετά approximates the Old Testament's use of עם in the sense of God's fellowship and companionship in giving help and aid.[115] It is unquestionable that "the use of χάρις at the beginning and end of the Pauline letters is much more than a mere polite cliche."[116] This use of χάρις testifies to both the continual need of God's gracious help and also His provision to meet that need. Similar is His use of χάρις in 1 Corinthians 15:10 where it is credited as the source of his ability to successfully labor in his ministry. In like manner, Paul appeals to Timothy to be continually strengthened for his ministry by the grace that is in Christ Jesus (2 Tim. 2:1) which Paul had found to be sufficient (2 Cor. 12:8-10). This use of χάρις is defined by Hendriksen as the "dynamic transforming operation of the Holy Spirit in their hearts."[117]

God is pictured as One who not only has given the

greatest gift but also continually gives to the believer. While the salutations and benedictions testify that the Christian life is a continual experience of the grace of God,[118] Paul does not speak of this continual aid of God's grace only in generalities. Specifically he mentions that Christian giving is a product of God's gracious work in the believer's life (2 Cor. 8:1, 6-7; 9:14) and that "the reward of giving is added grace"[119] (2 Cor. 9:8). Likewise, the continual instruction and training that God gives to His children in leading them step by step is stated to be a product of the grace of God (Titus 2:12). The present participle παιδεύουσα is from the same stem as the noun pedagogue and is broad enough to include instruction, encouragement, comforting, convicting, restraining, and discipline.[120]

<u>In the giving of spiritual gifts</u>. A further display of God's grace is seen in that God's grace is the basis for His giving each believer a spiritual gift (Rom. 12:3, 6; Eph. 4:7). The term χάρισμα is also employed to underscore this display of God's grace (Rom. 1:11, 12:6; 1 Cor. 1:7, 12:4, 9, 28, 30-31; 1 Tim. 4:14; 2 Tim. 1:6).

<u>Description of God's grace</u>

<u>Sufficient</u>. "The grace of God is for Paul 'radiant adequacy.'"[121] God declared His grace to be sufficient and the perfect tense--εἴρηκεν--notes the abiding significance of God's statement in 2 Corinthians 12:9. Likewise, it is

one's weakness that displays the sufficiency of this grace and for this reason Paul was well content with weakness and difficulties (2 Cor. 12:10) and even boasted in them (2 Cor. 12:5, 9). The grace of God is described as the "surpassing grace of God" (2 Cor. 9:14) in that it so abounds to the believer that his needs are not only completely met but also his life is enabled to abound in every good work (2 Cor. 9:8). As Hughes puts it, "God's giving of His grace is the complete opposite of grudging and forced."[122] The sufficiency of God's grace to triumph over sin is noted by the πολλῷ μᾶλλον and ἐπερίσσευσεν in Romans 5:15, μολλῷ μᾶλλον and περισσείαν in Romans 5:17, and is climaxed by the ὑπερεπερίσσευσεν of Romans 5:20. Paul personalizes this triumph of God's grace in noting that it was more than abundant in his own experience (1 Tim. 1:14). It is fitting that it is also called the grace that surpasses riches (Eph. 2:7). Hendriksen makes this observation about Paul's teaching of the sufficiency of God's grace:

> As Paul sees it, there is nothing narrow about this grace of God, nothing stingy. Its loving arms embrace both Gentile and Jew. It reaches even to 'the chief of sinners' (Paul himself) and so 'rich' is it that it enriches every heart and life which it touches, filling it with marvelous love, joy, peace, etc.[123]

<u>Unmerited</u>. "The essence of the doctrine of grace is that God is for us. What is more, he is for us who in ourselves are against him."[124] The principle of grace as noted by κατὰ χάριν (Rom. 4:4) is viewed in antithesis to the

principle of works which is noted by κατὰ ὀφείλημα (Rom. 4:4) and ἐξ ἔργων (Rom. 11:6). While χάρις already had the connotation of "a bestowal of help by an act of one's generosity,"[125] Christianity heightened this concept beyond one's highest imagination. Paul underscores this truth by combining δωρέαν with χάρις in Romans 3:24 and χαριτόω with χάρις in Ephesians 1:6 as if to stack up his terms in order to more forcefully assert the unmerited nature of grace. This truth seems to never escape Paul's mind (1 Cor. 15:10; 1 Tim. 1:14), who found it so amazing having so zealously operated on the merit principle (Phil. 3:4-6).

Righteous. While God's grace is not merited by man, it is merited for man by Jesus Christ. The God who justifies the sinner by grace through Christ's work manifests both His justice and His grace at the same time (Rom. 3:24-26). It is for this reason that grace is said to reign through righteousness (Rom. 5:21).

Sovereign. Paul emphasizes the freedom of the exercise of God's grace. The very essence of grace is that it is free. As Parker says, "If grace were an obligation on God's part, it would no longer be grace."[126] It is not dependent on anything outside of His attributes.

Distinction between God's grace and mercy

One should not press the similarity between these

two attributes to the extent that the distinction between the two is obliterated. The mention of the two in such close proximity argues for a distinction that is more than stylistic (Eph. 2:4, 7-8; 1 Tim. 1:13-14; Titus 3:5, 7). The two attributes are closely related but have a different focus. The focus of God's grace is the favor that He shows to those who have broken His law and deserve His wrath. The focus of God's mercy is the compassion that He shows to those in misery and distress.[127] In the divine mind His mercy precedes His grace, but in the manifestation of these His grace precedes His mercy.[128]

The Kindness of God

The lexical basis

The revelation of this attribute in Paul's writings centers around his use of χρηστός and χρηστότης. Χρηστός, which was originally a verbal adjective of χρῆσθαι, "to take into use," denoted usefulness in the sense of that which was suitable and proper.[129] It could refer to an "orderly" house or "tasty" food.[130] In relationship to people it could refer to one who was particularly useful in a specific function or trade,[131] but more generally denoted "moral excellence and perfection, in which inner greatness was linked with genuine goodness of heart" and "the capacity to show kindness to everyone."[132] Χρηστότης was used only to characterize people and denoted friendliness, kindness, and mildness.[133] It was a title of honor for a ruler or important public figure.[134] In the LXX, χρηστός refers to things or people, but its most characteristic use is in reference to the praise and worship of God.[135] Χρηστότης in the LXX is almost exclusively used in reference to God and with only one exception it is confined to the Psalms.[136] Both are used primarily to translate טוב and in relation to God denote His kindly disposition and the gifts that flow from this kindness.[137] Outside the LXX these words were only very rarely used in relationship to deity as this virtue did not seem to be appropriate to the divine majesty.[138] Χρηστός occurs seven times in the New Testament and χρηστότης occurs ten times. The former is found three times in Paul and the latter is exclusively Pauline.

Display of the kindness of God

Providential Care. God's kindness is linked with His forbearance and patience in Romans 2:4, and Paul singles out kindness as the attribute that leads one to repentance. Barclay comments on the use of χρηστός in Romans 2:4 by noting:

> There are two words for 'good' in Greek; there is 'agathos' and there is 'chrēstos.' The difference between them is this. The goodness of a man who is 'agathos' may well issue in rebuke and discipline and punishment; but the goodness of a man who is 'chrēstos' is always essentially kind. Jesus was 'agathos' when He cleansed the Temple and drove the money-changers and the sellers of doves from it in the white heat of His anger. Jesus was 'chrēstos' when He treated with loving gentleness the sinning woman who anointed His feet, or the woman taken in adultery.[139]

Trench comes to the same conclusion in noting that χρηστότης denotes the absence of harshness and cites Matthew 11:30 as an example.[140] Likewise, it is used in antithesis of God's severity in Romans 11:22.

How does God manifest His kindness in His providential care? It includes His temporarily withholding judgment, but this is primarily underscored by the "patience" and "forbearance" of Romans 2:4. The kind treatment of God also includes what Paul declares in his speech at Lystra. He refers in Acts 14:17 to God's doing good, sending rain, giving fruitful seasons, and to His satisfying their hearts with food and gladness as a witness to the nations.[141] This χρηστότης, which has been defined as "benignity and sweetness such as invites to familiar intercourse and sweet converse and bestows all manner of good"[142] or more simply as God's "kindness, benevolence, benignity, and disposition to bless,"[143] is designed to lead one to repentance. This kindness is designed to show "our duty toward a Being who is so kind, and . . . to give a ground to hope for our acceptance."[144] Paul's teaching on this display of God's kindness is in keeping with Jesus' teaching that God is kind to ungrateful and evil men (Luke 6:45).

<u>In provision of salvation</u>. Titus 3:4 states that the kindness of God "has appeared." Ἐπεφάνη, which also occurs in Titus 2:14, notes that this quality of God was "always there but received a clear manifestation in the coming of Christ and the consequent proclamation of the gospel."[145]

It is linked with God's love in Titus 3:4 and as Hiebert states, "Glimpses of these characteristics had been given in the Old Testament, but it was especially in the proclamation of the Gospel that there was announced to the world this benignity of 'God our Saviour.'"[146] This kindness of God in relation to God's provision of salvation in Christ is seen in Ephesians 2:7 as that attribute which in a special way will be on eternal display. In Romans 11:22 God's kindness is viewed as the fountain from which all the blessings and riches of salvation in God's sovereign plan have flowed to the Gentiles. The stern exhortation to continue in this kindness denotes not only a responsibility for the believer but also a promise that there is this provision of God's kindness that one can cling to as he continues in it. The kind provision of salvation in Christ far excells any Greek idea of χρηστότης that might be "ascribed to some earthly ruler upon whom the praises of men are being showered, praises which he has hardly deserved; but here is the 'real' benignity and love."[147] It is only God's Spirit who can produce this quality in man (Gal. 5:22; Eph. 4:32; Col. 3:12).

Description of the kindness of God

Abundant. In characteristic Pauline style this attribute is referred to by the phrase τοῦ πλούτου τῆς χρηστότητος αὐτοῦ (Rom. 2:4). The πλούτου underscores the abundant nature of God's resources of kindness and the value of the gifts that flow from His kindness.[148]

Unmerited. The context where the kindness of God is stated to have appeared describes man as foolish, disobedient, deceived, enslaved to various lusts and pleasures, and engaged in a life of malice, envy, and hate (Titus 3:3-4). It is the transforming nature of this kindness in Christ that can remake a person who does no kindness (Rom. 3:12) into one who is uncontentious, gentle, and shows every consideration for all human beings (Titus 3:2).

Misunderstood. Man is prone to take lightly the riches of God's kindness in thinking that he has merited it and falsely reasoning that he will escape God's judgment. It is for this reason that God's wrath and severity are viewed as the consequence of those who think lightly of God's kindness.[149]

The Patience of God

The lexical basis

The terms ἀνοχή and μακροθυμία are used by Paul to describe this attribute of God. The former was used commonly in classical Greek and for the most part signifies "a truce or suspension of arms."[150] It occurs only once in the LXX (1 Macc. 12:25) and carries the "purely temporal sense of 'delay.'"[151] It occurs only twice in the New Testament and both uses are in Paul in reference to God's forbearance (Rom. 2:4, 3:25). Ἀνέχομαι, the corresponding verb, also occurs in Paul but not directly in relation to God.

Μακροθυμία and its cognates can be described as comparatively late and rare in non-biblical Greek.[152] It is used strictly as a human virtue, "for whereas the gods know nothing of affliction, man has to bear his lot in patience."[153] It is also true that "in ancient Greece μακροθυμία is concerned primarily with the molding of a man's own character; it is not a virtue exercised toward one's fellows."[154] In noting the use of this term in the LXX, it can be said that "the word takes on a distinctive depth in biblical usage."[155] The adjective μακρόθυμος frequently denotes an attribute of Yahweh and the phrase ארך אפים is often rendered by μακροθυμία and μακρόθυμος.[156] The word is therefore "inseparably linked with the idea of restrained wrath, forbearance being exercised for a limited period only."[157] It is also used as a human virtue in the LXX (Prov. 14:29, 16:32, 19:11, 25:15). Of the fourteen uses of μακροθυμία in the New Testament, ten occur in Paul. Of these ten, three are a direct reference to God (Rom. 2:4, 9:22; 1 Tim. 1:16); and the other seven refer to this quality which God desires to produce in the believer (2 Cor. 6:6; Gal. 5:22; Eph. 4:2; Col. 1:11, 3:12; 2 Tim. 3:10, 4:2). The corresponding verb μακροθυμέω is used twice by Paul (1 Cor. 13:4; 1 Thess. 5:14).

Ἀνοχή is forbearance that is temporary and transient and "after a certain lapse of time, and unless other conditions intervene, it will pass away."[158] While this is also true of μακροθυμία, this temporary and provisional character of the forbearance does not lie in the word.[159] A related word is ὑπομονή, which is used of patience in regard to things, as opposed to μακροθυμία, which expresses a patience that is in respect to persons. While both are a necessary virtue for man, only μακροθυμία is an attribute of God. The rebellious wills of men do provoke God, but there is no resistance or burden upon Him from things. God is called the θεὸς τῆς ὑπομονῆς only in the sense that He gives this quality to His people (Rom. 15:5).[160]

Display of the patience of God

In dealing with pre-cross sins. In Romans 3:25 it is stated that it was God's forbearance that led Him to pass over the sins that had been previously committed before the death of Christ.[161] One of the purposes of the cross was to demonstrate His righteousness lest this forbearance be misunderstood (Rom. 3:25). As Horst has stated, "God's patience does not overlook anything. It simply sees further than man. It has the end in view. It has the true insight that knows best."[162]

In delaying the final judgment. The purpose of the present display of God's patience is that it may give man additional time to repent and flee from his coming wrath and run to His mercy (Rom. 2:4-5, 11:22-23; cf. 2 Peter 3:9). It is for this reason that His judgment is delayed.

In the salvation of Paul. As God endures the provocations of the sins of men, His forbearance is seen. However, were it not for Paul's own example, one would not be able to discern "the whole of God's longsuffering"[163] (1 Tim. 1:16). Instead of promptly striking down this blasphemer and persecutor, the Lord bore with him and kept on bearing with him until he became an object of His mercy, and by so doing provided an "example" to all future believers. Paul in turn sought to exemplify it in his life (2 Cor. 6:6; 2 Tim. 3:10) and prayed that this quality would also characterize his converts (Col. 1:11, 3:12; Eph. 4:2).

Description of God's patience

Abundant. The abundance of God's patience is brought out by the πολλῇ in Romans 9:22 as well as by the supreme demonstration of God's patience in the salvation of Paul (1 Tim. 1:16). Wrath and mercy are the two boundaries which constitute the span of God's patience.[164] As Barclay has written:

> If God had been a man he would long ago have taken his hand and, with a gesture, would have wiped out the world, but in his 'patience' he bears with the sins, the follies, and the disobedience of men. The great obligation which rests on the Christian is just this--he must be as patient with his fellow-men as God has been with him.[165]

Despised. Paul warns men against despising or thinking lightly of this attribute (Rom. 2:4). It is despised when one does not use the opportunity, made possible by God's delay in judgment, to flee to God's mercy in repentance.[166]

The Truthfulness and Faithfulness of God

The lexical basis

The key words that are used in the revelation of this attribute are ἀλήθεια, ἀληθής, ἀληθινός, πίστις, and πιστός. In classical Greek ἀλήθεια primarily denoted truth in contrast to mere appearance and especially carried this meaning in Greek philosophy. In a more general sense it could simply denote the truth in contrast to the telling of a lie or deceitful flattery.[167] Ἀληθής, likewise, could be used to contrast reality from the realm of mere appearance but also in a less metaphysical way denoted the true facts of a matter.[168] Ἀληθίνος frequently meant "real" or "genuine" but could also simply mean "truthful."[169] The key Hebrew word which is used in relationship to this word group in the LXX is אמת, which primarily carried the idea of reliability or faithfulness but also could denote truthfulness in contrast to falsehood.[170] It is only the passive meaning of πίστις and πιστός that is particularly relevant to this study, and their meaning of reliability and faithfulness is attested in the classical use of each.[171] In the LXX πίστις is used chiefly for אמונה which denoted firmness, faithfulness, fidelity, and in relation to God denoted His total dependability.[172] Πιστός is used chiefly for נאמן, which also denoted that which was reliable and trustworthy.[173] The use of these words in Paul's writing is developed in the display of this attribute.

Display of the truthfulness and faithfulness of God

In His providing a revelation. Ἀληθεία is a term that is used by Paul to denote the revelation of God. It is used of His revelation in creation (Rom. 1:18, 25), in the Law (Rom. 2:20), and especially of the revelation of the truth of the gospel (Gal. 2:5, 14, 5:7; Eph. 1:13; Col. 1:5). It is through this revelation that man could know the ultimate realities of life. Furthermore, it is of course only a truthful God who can author a revelation that contains absolute truth (cf. 2 Cor. 1:18). "Without truth in God, a revelation is only a mockery."[174]

In being true to His revelation. In Paul's writings the corresponding fact of God's truthfulness to His revelation is likewise clearly emphasized. The use of ἀληθεία in Romans 15:8 and perhaps in Romans 3:7 carries this idea of God's faithfulness to His revelation.[175] The meaning of ἀληθής in Romans 3:4 also denotes God's reliability and trustworthiness[176] as does the πίστις of Romans 3:3.[177] God is true to His revelation and all the promises that it contains as the ἀψευδής of Titus 1:2 refers to Him as the "un-lie-able God"[178] or the God who cannot lie. It is for this reason that any statement that represents God's truth is a "trustworthy statement" (1 Tim. 1:15, 3:1, 4:9; 2 Tim. 2:11; Titus 3:8) and a "faithful" word (Titus 1:9) because it can be relied on. God's revelation is a priceless treasure because

God is a reliable God who is not given to fickleness.

In His judgments. The οἴδαμεν of Romans 2:4 declare it to be a fact of common knowledge that God's judgments are "right." Κατὰ ἀλήθειαν in this verse declares that God will judge according to truth and therefore justly.[179]

In contrasting Himself to idols. God is the true God in the sense that He is real and genuine as opposed to an idol which has no reality. God is the opposite of all that is "fictitious, counterfeit, imaginary, simulated, and pretended."[180] It is this idea that the Apostle Paul had in mind when he spoke in Athens (Acts 17:29, cf. 1 Thess 1:9).

In Christ. God displays His faithfulness and truthfulness in the sending of His Son (Rom. 15:8). Also in Christ is the very embodiment of God's truth (Eph. 4:21; cf. John 14:6).[181]

In His dealing with Israel. God's faithfulness and truthfulness is seen in His dealings with the nation Israel. In addition to the terms in Romans 3:3 and 3:4 that have already been noted is the use of ἀμεταμέλητος in Romans 11:29. In connection with this verse Murray observes:

> 'The gifts and the calling of God' have reference to those mentioned in Romans 9:4, 5 as the privileges and prerogatives of Israel. That these 'are not repented of' is expressly to the effect that the adoption, the covenants, and the promises in their relation to Israel have not been abrogated.[182]

In His dealing with His church. The church is the pillar and support of God's truth in that it upholds it before the world and supports it in spite of opposition (1 Tim. 3:15).[183] The church is not only the recipient of God's truth but is also in living relation with the God of truth. The believer's confidence toward the future and the consummation of his salvation is based on the faithfulness of God (1 Cor. 1:9). Likewise, it is an attribute that the believer can count on in temptation and spiritual conflict. It is the faithful God who will give a way of escape to allow one to endure a temptation, and who will strengthen and protect the believer from Satan (1 Cor. 10:13; 2 Thess. 3:3).[184] Paul was convinced that in all matters God could be trusted (cf. 2 Tim. 1:12). As an imitator of God (Eph. 5:1) Paul lived by this standard of truthfulness (cf. Rom. 9:1; 2 Cor. 7:14, 11:10, 12:6; Gal. 1:20; 1 Tim. 2:7) and faithfulness (2 Cor. 1:18) and encouraged his converts to do the same (1 Cor. 4:2, 5:8; Eph. 4:25).

In His reaction to man's unbelief and unfaithfulness. While men may suppress God's truth or exchange it in order to embrace their lies (Rom. 1:18, 25), the God of truth and His revelation are not affected. Paul asserts that the unfaithfulness of men cannot alter the faithfulness of God (Rom. 3:3). In fact if every man were a liar, this would not change the fact that God is true (Rom. 3:4). God displays His truthfulness and faithfulness by necessarily remaining faithful in spite of man's unbelief and unfaithfulness. This shows the infinite nature of this attribute in God. Men can trust God to build this quality in their lives and such was the case of Timothy (1 Cor. 4:17), Paul (1 Cor. 7:25; 1 Tim. 1:12), Tychicus (Eph. 6:21; Col. 4:7), Epaphras (Col. 1:7), and Onesimus (Col. 4:9); but it is only necessarily true of God alone. Even a faithful man can become momentarily unfaithful out of desire, fear, weakness, lack of interest, or some outward influence. However, in all circumstances God remains faithful because He cannot deny Himself (2 Tim. 2:13).

The Righteousness of God

The lexical basis

The key terms in Paul's writings that denote this attribute are δίκαιος and δικαιοσύνη. In the Greek world δίκαιος referred to the one conformed to the standards of society, one who fulfills his obligations to man or God, and as a legal term one "who observes legal norms."[185] It became a leading term in ethics.[186] It was later broadened to note the conformity to any standard, and thus it could note a carriage that ran smoothly or a speech that was appropriate.[187] Δικαιοσύνη denoted the character of the δίκαιος. It therefore, denoted the quality of conforming to a standard and is used for justice which was the business of a judge.[188] In the LXX they are primarily used to translate צדיק and צדקה respectively. It is here that they became firmly linked to the character and judgment of God and the norm or standard is God's revealed character. Previously they only rarely referred to the divine and the standard was primarily that of social obligation.[189] In Paul δικαίος is used in regard to men in noting the universal absence of those who fit in this category on their own merit (Rom. 3:10), in denoting those whom God has declared righteous (Rom. 5:19), and in denoting one's ethical character (Titus 1:8). It is also used to signify what is right whether in regard to one's actions (Eph. 6:1; Col. 4:1) or one's thoughts (Phil. 1:7, 4:8). It is the use of δίκαιος in relation to God that is most germane to this study. It refers to His manifested character (Rom. 3:26), His Law (Rom. 7:12), and His judgment (2 Thess. 1:5-6; 2 Tim. 4:8). Δικαιοσύνη is used to refer to the character of God (Rom. 3:5), the gift of righteousness to the believer (Rom. 5:17), and the standard for the believer's life (Rom. 6:18). The use of these terms in Paul's writings is further developed in discussing the display of God's righteousness.

The display of the righteousness of God

Some such as Reumann,[190] Schmid,[191] Myers,[192] and Weiss,[193] see the righteousness of God as the central theme in Paul's theology. At the very least one is able to agree with Guthrie who states, "In the NT the Apostle Paul is the great exponent of this important characteristic of God."[194] In Paul it is not technically correct to say that justice requires God to do a certain thing. God is free to act as He wills and this will of necessity always be righteous because He is righteous. Therefore, while there is no law above God, there is a law in God in that He is bound by His nature as He conforms to the standard of His own character.[195] The emphasis in Paul is on the revelation and demonstration of God's righteousness (Rom. 1:17, 3:25). It is not seen or discussed as a static quality but as one that is dynamic and active in the world.

<u>In His impartial judgment</u>. The principle of God's righteous judgment is seen in Romans 2:6 when he "echoes the language of Ps. 62:12"[196] in noting that God will render to every man according to his deeds. The same principle is found in Paul's use of the Hebraism λαμβάνειν πρόσωπον in Galatians 2:6 and his three uses of the corresponding noun προσωποληµψία which arose out of it (Rom. 2:11; Eph. 6:9; Col. 3:25).[197] It denotes the impartiality with which God judges, for the Hebraism "to receive face" means "to base one's judgment and action on external and irrelevant considerations."[198] The Hebrew equivalent נשא פנים referred to the practice of the Oriental greeting when one would turn his face to the ground and if the person greeted raised his bowed face it was a sign of recognition and esteem.[199] However, God is such a God that He is not a respecter of persons. He judges slaves and masters (Eph. 6:9; Col. 3:25), Jew and Gentile (Rom. 2:11; cf. 11:21), and in summary every man

(Rom. 2:6) with no partiality, and His judgment cannot be corrupted.[200] In addition to Romans 2:6 and the truth that God is not a respecter of persons is the idea in Paul that God cannot be mocked (Ga. 6:7). Μυκτηρίζω occurs only in Galatians 6:7 in the New Testament and in this context carries the idea of "outwitting."[201] The present tense is gnomic[202] and therefore presents a timeless truth. The truth it teaches is that "it is vain to expect to outwit God by reaping a harvest different from that which one has sown."[203] Guthrie's words are a fitting summary as he states, "An absolutely righteous God must judge in an absolutely righteous way (cf. Rom. 2:5)."[204]

In His condemnation of the sinner. The righteous judgment of God is displayed in both His condemning men and in His justifying them. The condemnation of men who pervert God's truth so as to promote evil is said to be just (Rom. 3:8). Paul emphatically denies the fact that God's infliction of wrath is in any way unrighteous by his characteristic μὴ γένοιτο (Rom. 3:5-6). In fact he declares that the future day of wrath will be a time in which the full exhibition of God's righteous judgment will be manifested (Rom. 2:5). In his speech at Athens he declared that the Son, Whom He had come to know as "The Righteous One," (Acts 22:14) will be the one through whom God will judge the world (Acts 17:31). The unrighteousness of men will serve to demonstrate His righteousness (Rom. 3:5).

In His justification of the believer. Paul speaks not only of the righteousness of God which punished sin but also of the justifying righteousness of God.[205] As Weiss states, "From his Pharisaic past, Paul had already brought with him the view, according to which everything depends in religion upon the realization of righteousness."[206] However, while Paul's past life had been characterized by the righteous external observance of the Law (Phil. 3:6), he had come to recognize himself as a member of God's rebellious race who lacked God's righteousness (Rom. 3:10) and who had to depend on God's gift of righteousness (Phil. 3:9). It is this to which Bruce refers as his "altered idea of God."[207] The righteousness of God is displayed in this gift of righteousness in that only an absolutely righteous God can give a gift of righteousness.[208] God is the justifier but His wise plan of salvation also declares Him to be just (Rom. 3:26).

In His revelation. God has displayed His righteousness in the revelation He has given to man. In Paul's writing this is seen in the universal moral law God has implanted in men's conscience (Rom. 2:14-15), in the Law that He has given to Israel (Rom. 7:12), and in the gospel message (Rom. 1:17).

In His dealings with the enemies of God's people. A particular way in which God's righteousness will be displayed is in His repaying with affliction those who have afflicted

His people (2 Thess. 1:6). As Hiebert states, "This assertion concerning the character of God and His judgment was intended to afford strong consolation to the afflicted readers."[209]

In His dealings with His children. The fact of this attribute is a focus of Paul's ethical instructions to believers (cf. Gal. 6:7; Eph. 6:9; Col. 3:25). Likewise, in Paul's teaching on rewards he notes that the One who distributes them is a "righteous Judge" (2 Tim. 4:8). The corresponding responsibility for the believer is to dedicate the members of his body as instruments of righteousness (Rom. 6:13) and to follow after righteousness (1 Tim. 6:11; 2 Tim. 2:22), which is his new master (Rom. 6:16, 18-19).

In His work of regeneration. While the body is dead because of sin, the spirit is alive because of righteousness (Rom. 8:10).[210] It is because of the righteousness of God that has been given to the believer as a gift that the Spirit of Christ indwells him and his spirit has been made alive by God's work of regeneration. This display of God's righteousness in His regenerating work is also seen in His creation of the new self in righteousness (Eph. 4:24).

In Christ's death. The death of Christ is said to have been a demonstration of God's righteousness (Rom. 3:25). In God's forbearance He had not dealt with the previously committed sins in a final way. The death of Christ served to demonstrate God's righteousness as it affirmed the fact that sin must be punished.

In vindicating His Son. The Son is said to have been justified or vindicated in the Spirit (1 Tim. 3:16). The phrase is a reference to "the vindication of His claims when God raised Him from the dead. Men rejected and crucified Him as a criminal but in the resurrection God reversed the verdict of men."[211] This action of God revealed the triumph of His righteousness over the unrighteous acts of men and is one of the places where δικαιόω means to declare to be right and this declaration carries no element of grace or pardon.[212]

In the public declaration of the believer's righteousness. In Galatians 5:5 righteousness is pictured as the object of the believer's hope.[213] The argument of the letter to the Galatians makes it extremely unlikely that this is a reference to initial justification which according to Paul is a present possession of a believer (cf. Rom. 5:1). This appears to be a reference to the future public declaration of the believer's righteousness at Christ's return.[214]

The holiness of God and the righteousness of God

It is the righteousness of God and not the holiness of God that is emphasized in Paul's writings. It is not that the latter is denied or doubted, but it is the expression of this holiness in God's dealing with man that is in the forefront in Paul's theology. While he clearly teaches that God is completely holy (1 Tim. 6:16),[215] the emphasis in Paul's writings is on the God who has appeared (Titus 2:11, 3:4). Ἁγίος is never used directly of God except as a title of the "Holy" Spirit.[216] Likewise, φῶς is never used directly of God as it is in John's writings.

The Wrath of God

"Wrath is an essential and inalienable trait in the biblical and NT view of God."[217] As Moule states, "All attempts to explain it away involves violence to the essence of Scripture: it would be as legitimate, in point of language, to explain away the Divine love."[218] An understanding of it is essential in apprehending an accurate conception of the Pauline view of God, who gives the "most careful and considered teaching on the subject of the divine wrath."[219]

The lexical basis

The primary word that Paul uses in discussing this truth about the character of God is ὀργή. In classical Greek it denoted one's temperament, disposition, and mood and could also denote anger or wrath.[220] In regard to the latter use, it could be positively evaluated as being in the service of righteousness and thus denote an appropriate attitude for a judge. However, it is mainly seen as a character defect in man.[221] It is also a prominent characteristic of the Greek and Roman gods.[222] In the LXX it is primarily used for אף,

חמה, חרון, עברה, קצף, זעם, and רגן. In regard to man it can refer to an anger that was justified (2 Sam. 12:5) or an outburst of anger that was regarded as a vice (Prov. 12:16, 27:3, 29:8). In regard to God, it is seen as His holy reaction against sin (Jer. 21:12). As Morris has said, "God is not thought of as capriciously angry (like the deities of the heathen), but because He is a moral being, His anger is directed toward wrongdoing in any shape or form."[223] In the same vein, Morris says, "There is a consistency about the wrath of God in the Old Testament. It is no capricious passion, but the stern reaction of the divine nature to evil in man."[224] God is pictured as the author of such wrath in personal terms, and it is not viewed as only an impersonal retribution (cf. Ps. 60:1-3; Isa. 30:27-31; Jer. 23:20; Ezek. 7:8ff.; Amos 3:6, 5:9). It should be added that the Old Testament teaching of God's wrath "must not be taken as a last word about God."[225] He gives prior warning before His wrath is exercised (Exod. 22:23ff., 32:10; Deut. 6:13ff.) and the truth of His being "slow to anger" is frequently taught as well as His desire to show mercy (cf. Jonah 3:10). In the New Testament ὀργή occurs thirty-six times and twenty-one of these occurrences are in Paul's writings.[226] It is used twelve times in Romans, and of these twelve no less than ten refer directly to God's wrath. In Paul it also can refer to a human sin (Eph. 4:31; Col. 3:8; 1 Tim. 2:8), although he does not regard all human anger as unjustified (Eph. 4:26;

cf. Rom. 13:4). The use of ὀργή in Paul is dealt with in more detail in the following sections.

While ὀργή is the most important word for the wrath of God, at least brief mention should be made of other words that contribute to the wrath of God in Paul. Θυμός occurs five times in Paul, but only once is it connected with divine wrath (Rom. 2:8). In distinguishing between θυμός and ὀργή, etymologically the former denotes more of an outburst of passion while the latter views anger as a settled indignation.[227] In the LXX[228] they are used synonymously and for this reason some have concluded that in the New Testament "there is no material difference between them."[229] It seems best to say that while the original distinction is not always observed between the two terms, ὀργή did lend itself as a more suitable term for divine wrath.[230] It is for this reason that θυμός is used for divine wrath only one time outside of the Apocalypse. Its use in the Apocalypse may be as Morris states in keeping with the vivid imagery of the book.[231] As Stahlin observes, "But one might very well say that θυμός, to which there clings the concept of passionate outburst, was well adapted for describing the visions of the seer, but not for delineating Paul's concept of the wrath of God."[232] The one use of θυμός in Paul that refers to God's wrath is found in Romans 2:8 where it occurs along with ὀργή. The combination "serves to emphasize the reality and the intensity of the divine displeasure poured out upon the ungodly in the day of righteous judgment."[233] In addition to θυμός, other words include ἐκδίκησις of Romans 12:19, which refers to God as the One who will execute revenge.[234] The corresponding ἔκδικος occurs in 1 Thessalonians 4:6. Finally, Paul's use of ἀποτομία in Romans 11:22 also contributes to the lexical basis of God's wrath. It denotes the severity of the divine judgment upon those who do not cleave to His goodness.[235]

The present display of God's wrath

The present display of God's wrath is discussed in Romans 1:18-32, and the fact of the present display or revelation of God's wrath is seen from the ἀποκαλύπτεται of Romans 1:18. As Lenski observes, "'Is revealed' is identical with 'is revealed' in v. 17, also in tense, and thus cannot refer only to the final revelation of wrath at the time of the last judgment, but must refer, first of all, to the revelation of wrath which is now in constant progress."[236] As Murray puts it, "The wrath of God is dynamically, effectively operative in the world of men . . . "[237] In the same vein he also states, "There is a positive outgoing of the divine displeasure."[238] The question revolves around the manner in which it is being displayed. Cranfield, who follows Barth, says that God's wrath is being revealed in the present proclamation of the gospel. Cranfield writes, "The preaching of Christ crucified, risen, ascended and coming again, is at the same time both the offer to men of a status of righteousness before God and the revelation of God's wrath against their sin."[239] Lenski takes it to refer to "the revelation that is found within man's own moral nature, his conscience, his sense of right and wrong, his feeling of responsibility and accountability, his sense of justice which assents to the punishment of all wrong."[240] Lenski writes, "The revelation of the wrath occurs in an endless succession, man's moral nature perceiving God's stern opposition in every punishment of sin."[241] While both of these interpretations are in line with scriptural truth, they do not take into account the verses that follow which "describe" God's action against ungodliness and unrighteousness. As Godet has said, "The idea of the 'revelation of divine wrath' is developed in vv. 24-27 . . . ."[242] In these verses one notes that παρέδωκεν is employed three times by the apostle in describing God's action.

Several points should be noted about this present display of wrath. First, the text explicitly emphasizes the just nature of God's action. This is seen from the use of διό of Romans 1:24, which refers back to the description of man's rejection of the truth of God as revealed in creation (Rom. 1:21-23). Liddon summarizes the process of Romans 1:21-23 as the practical indifference to God's truth, intrinsically worthless speculation about God, disappearance of the idea of God from the minds of men, pride of philosophy which coincides with spiritual and moral folly, and fetishism.[243] The just nature of God's action is also underscored by the διὰ τοῦτο of Romans 1:26 and the καθὼς of Romans 1:28. Secondly, it is an action that on the one hand is not God forcing them to do evil, which would be contrary to His holiness, and on the other hand the active verb does not only signify a passive permission. It involves a positive withdrawal of His restraining help and a handing over to a greater intensity of sin.[244] Godet sees an element of mercy involved in the action by noting that "when man has reached a certain degree of corruption, he can only be cured by the very excess of his own corruption; it is the only means left of producing what all preceding appeals and punishments failed to effect, the salutary action of repentance."[245] The withdrawal of restraint is apparently not total in light of Romans 1:32. Those who have been "given up" still know that the practice of sin merits God's judgment. In relation to Romans 1:32, Hodge observes that "the judicial abandonment of God does not destroy the free agency or responsibility of men."[246] Thirdly, the passage teaches that this punishment is manifested in the moral degradation of men which can take a variety of forms with homosexuality being one of the most extreme cases. Fourthly, this abandonment involves not only the practice of sin but also an approval of it.

In addition to this key passage, there is also a present display of God's wrath to the evildoer through the instrumentality of human government (Rom. 13:4). As Cranfield says, "Through the state there takes place a partial, anticipatory, provisional manifestation of God's wrath against sin."[247] Such is the present display of God's wrath in Paul's writings.

The future display of God's wrath

The future display of God's wrath is seen in Romans 5:9 where Paul states that the believer will be saved from it. 'Οργή in Romans 5:9 refers to "the wrath that will be dispensed to the ungodly at the day of judgment, the eschatological wrath."[248] In Romans 2:5 this future display of God's wrath is called the "day of wrath and the revelation of the righteous judgment of God." It is called the "coming wrath" in 1 Thessalonians 1:10. In this verse ἐκ τῆς οργῆς τῆς ἐρχομένης probably refers to both the wrath of God displayed in the tribulation and the eternal wrath. Such is the conclusion of Stahlin when he writes, "There are two points in the future where eschatological ὀργή has a place, first in the tribulation before the end, then in the final judgment itself."[249] In the other references that have been cited the wrath of the tribulation may be included (cf. 1 Thess. 5:9), but the primary focus of Romans 2:5, 2:8, and 5:9 is on the eternal wrath of God.

The objects of God's wrath

The doctrine of man in Paul's writings includes the

truth that men are by nature children of wrath (Eph. 2:3). The φύσει of Ephesians 2:3 contrasts what man innately is to what he is by God's grace (cf. Eph. 2:5, 8). The phrase τέκνα ὀργῆς of Ephesians 2:3 is "a Semitism to denote those who deserve God's punishment."[250] Furthermore, the objects of God's wrath are stated to be all ungodliness and unrighteous (Rom. 1:18); those who despise His kindness, forbearance, and patience (Rom. 2:4); the stubborn and unrepentant (Rom. 2:5); those who are selfishly ambitious and obey unrighteousness rather than the truth (Rom. 2:8); every one who does evil (Rom. 2:9); sons of disobedience (Eph. 5:6); specific sins of the flesh (Col. 3:5-6); the enemies of God's people (Rom. 12:19-21; 2 Thess. 1:6); and those who do not know God and those who do not obey the gospel (2 Thess. 1:8).

In summarizing the above phrases, it can first be noted that God's wrath is universal in that His holy displeasure is directed against "all" ungodliness and unrighteousness. Secondly, it can be noted that sin is described both generally and specifically. In general terms it is described as ungodliness, "an attack on the majesty of God," and unrighteousness, "a violation of God's just order."[251] Paul describes it more specifically in such passages as Romans 1:29-32; 1 Corinthians 5:11, 6:9-10; 2 Corinthians 12:20; Galatians 5:19-21; Ephesians 4:31, 5:3-4; and Colossians 3:5-9. Thirdly, there is a connection between the rejection of God's revelation and the corresponding manifestation of sin, whether it be His revelation in creation (Rom. 1:18-20) or in the gospel (2 Thess. 1:8).

Character of God's wrath

The emphasis in Paul is on the righteous and eternal character of God's wrath. The righteous character of God's wrath is seen from the denial of any ἀδικία in it (Rom. 3: 5-6), the use of the term δικαιοκρισίας in Romans 2:5, and the use of δίκαιος in 2 Thessalonians 1:6. God's wrath is declared to be righteous and not capricious or arbitrary. It is not an uncontrollable outburst of passion. As Hurst notes, "The fact that μακροθυμία stands alongside God's ὀργή means that this ὀργή is freed from anthropomorphic misunderstanding."[252] Bedenbaugh notes "that there is no exact counterpart in human personality."[253] The eternal nature of God's wrath is seen from the use of αἰώνιον in 2 Thessalonians 1:9. As Hiebert notes, "This adjective is derived from the noun αἰών, 'an age, a period of undefined duration,' hence αἰώνιος denotes 'age-long,' whatever the length of the period."[254] Of its some seventy uses in the New Testament only on three occasions is it used of a period that is not endless.[255] Since in 2 Thessalonians 1:9 it refers to the age to come, it denotes that which is eternal and everlasting. Thayer maintains that the term "gives prominence to the immeasurableness of eternity."[256] It is the same term that Paul uses to denote eternal life (Rom. 2:7, 5:21, 6:22-23; Gal. 6:8; 2 Thess. 2:16; 1 Tim. 1:16, 6:12, 19; Titus 1:2,

3:7) and the eternality of God (Rom. 16:26).

In regard to the character of God's wrath, it should also be noted that it should not be understood merely as an impersonal force at work in the world.[257] It is true that fifteen of the eighteen uses of ὀργή in Paul do not have the corresponding genitive θεοῦ. However, this should not distort the fact that the genitive is specifically mentioned in Romans 1:18, Ephesians 5:6, and Colossians 3:6. As Stahlin puts it, "The common absence of θεοῦ does not support the conclusion that even Paul felt ὀργή to be an independent hypostasis. It simply shows us how strong was the awareness of God in all things."[258] In a similar way χάρις often occurs without the genitive, and it is self-evident that the reference is to the grace of God. Paul's teaching of the display of the wrath of God does not view God merely as a spectator. Morris states:

> The God of the New Testament does not sit back and let 'natural' laws bring about the defeat of evil. He is actively opposed to evil in every shape and form. Where unpleasant consequences follow on evil-doing His hand is in it.[259]

To the same effect Guthrie notes, "It is not sufficient to define wrath as the principle of retribution in a moral universe without connecting the principle to its source, i.e., to the nature of God."[260]

Rather than being an impersonal force, God's wrath is "something habitual and natural in God"[261] and indicates His displeasure of evil, His passionate resistance to all rebellion against His authority, and His corresponding judgment.[262] It is a divine attitude but divine anger is not any more rage than divine love is lust.[263] Is this attribute consistent with His love? It is not only consistent but a necessary part of His love. God could not be a loving God if He did not react to evil. Guthrie makes this point when he writes, "Some concept of wrath is needed to safeguard the purity of divine love."[264] Prat observes, "God hates sin in the same proportion as he loves moral order--namely, infinitely."[265] Likewise, Morris says:

> There is a divine love, but it is not a careless sentimentality indifferent to the moral integrity of the loved ones. Rather it is a love which is a purifying fire, blazing against everything that hinders the loved ones from being the very best that they can be.[266]

The opposite of expressing God's wrath is the experience of His salvation (1 Thess. 5:9). Paul had learned that this salvation is not found in the Law which brings about wrath (Rom. 4:15) but in Christ who is called "The Deliverer" from the coming wrath (1 Thess. 1:10) and in Whom the experience of this salvation from God's wrath is certain (Rom. 5:9).

Notes

[1]Cremer notes that this corresponds to John's assertion that "God is love" (1 John 4:8). Hermann Cremer, *Biblico-Theological Lexicon of New Testament Greek*, p. 15.

[2]James S. Stewart, *A Man in Christ--The Vital Elements of St. Paul's Religion*, p. 40. Also see Leon Morris, "Paul, Apostle of Love," *Christianity Today* 21 (September 1977): 76, 78.

[3]Henry C. Sheldon, *New Testament Theology*, p. 200.

[4]*A Theological Word Book of the Bible*, s.v. "Love," by C. E. B. Cranfield, p. 133.

[5]*TNIDNTT*, s.v. "ἀγαπάω," by W. Gunther and H. G. Link, 2 (1976):539. There was also a mystical connotation of ἔρως that described the desire of the worshiper to unite with the divine.

[6]Ibid.

[7]Henry Liddell and George Scott, *A Greek-English Lexicon*, s.v. "στοργέω," p. 1650.

[8]William Barclay, *New Testament Words*, p. 18.

[9]Ibid.

[10]John uses it to denote the Father's love for the Son (John 5:20), Jesus' love for Lazarus (John 11:3, 36), Father's love for the disciples (John 16:27), Jesus' love for John (John 20:2), and Christ's love for the church (Rev. 3:19).

[11]*TDNT*, s.v. "ἀγαπάω," by Ethelbert Stauffer, 1 (1964):37.

[12]Ibid., 1 (1964):36.

[13]Liddell and Scott, s.v. "ἀγαπάω," p. 6.

[14]Barclay, p. 19.

[15]*TDNT*, s.v. "ἀγαπάω," by Ethelbert Stauffer, 1 (1964):37.

[16]Ibid., 1 (1964):36.   [17]Ibid., 1 (1964):37.

[18]Ernest DeWitt Burton, A Critical and Exegetical Commentary on the Epistle to the Galatians, ICC, p. 519.

[19]Hermann Cremer, Biblico-Theological Lexicon of New Testament Greek, p. 14.

[20]Barclay, p. 20.

[21]A Theological Word Book of the Bible, s.v. "Love," by C. E. B. Cranfield, p. 134.

[22]James Moulton and George Milligan, The Vocabulary of the Greek Testament, s.v. "ἀγαπάω," p. 2.

[23]Ibid. It is true that ἀγαπάω is not always sharply distinct from φιλέω, especially in John's writings. However, the former is almost exclusively used in Paul's writings for God's love with the only exception being the use of φιλανθρωπία in Titus 3:4.

[24]W. E. Vine, An Expository Dictionary of New Testament Words, 4 vols., 3:21.

[25]A Theological Word Book of the Bible, s.v. "Love," by C. E. B. Cranfield, p. 134.

[26]Herman Cremer, Biblico-Theological Lexicon of New Testament Greek, p. 15.

[27]Examples of συνίστημι having the force of demonstrate include Romans 3:5, 2 Corinthians 6:4, 7:11, and Galatians 2:18.

[28]D. Edmond Hiebert, Titus and Philemon, EBC, p. 69.

[29]Homer A. Kent, Jr., The Pastoral Epistles, p. 241.

[30]H. C. G. Moule, Studies in Colossians and Philemon, KPG, p. 75.

[31]Willibald Beyschlag, New Testament Theology or Historical Account of the Teaching of Jesus and of Primitive Christianity according to New Testament Sources, p. 93.

[32]James Moffatt, Love in the New Testament, p. 151.

[33]TNIDNTT, s.v. "ἀγαπάω," by W. Gunther and H. G. Link, 2 (1976):539.

[34]Ibid.

[35] D. Edmond Hiebert, The Thessalonian Epistles, p. 50.

[36] Τὴν ἐκλογὴν ὑμων in 1 Thess. 1:4; εἵλατο ὑμᾶς in 2 Thess. 2:13: and ἐκλεκτοί in Colossians 3:12. Ridderbos says that "'Beloved' is used synonymously with elect by Paul . . ." Herman Ridderbos, Paul--An Outline of His Theology, p. 332.

[37] John Murray, The Epistle to the Romans, NTC, 2 vols., 2:101.

[38] Moffatt, p. 139.

[39] H. A. A. Kennedy, The Theology of the Epistles, p. 135.

[40] TNIDNTT, s.v. "ἀγαπάω," by W. Gunther and H. G. Link, 2 (1976):545.

[41] The most striking reference to God's electing love is in Romans 9:13 because of the use of μισέω. Paul is quoting from Malachi 1:2-5. Ἐμίσησα may have the Semitic sense of "love less" (cf. Gen. 29:31-33; Deut. 21:15; Matt. 6:24, 10:37-38; Luke 14:26; John 12:25) and in the context of Romans 9 would refer to Esau and perhaps his descendants (Edom) not being chosen.

[42] The standard for the believer's life who is to be an imitator of God (Eph. 5:1) is that all of his activities are to be motivated by love (1 Cor. 13:1-3, 16:14; 1 Thess. 1:3). Likewise, they are to bring glory to God (1 Cor. 10:31).

[43] W. E. Vine, An Expository Dictionary of New Testament Words, 4 vols., 3:21

[44] This is part of the force of Paul's statement in Philippians 1:21--"for to me to live is Christ." The statement is pregnant enough to also include the ideas of Philippians 3:10 and 4:13.

[45] TDNT, s.v. "ἀγαπάω," by Ethelbert Stauffer, 1 (1964):50.

[46] TNIDNTT, s.v. "ἀγαπάω," by W. Gunther and H. G. Link, 2 (1976):545.

[47] William Hendriksen, Exposition of Ephesians, NTC, p. 173.

[48] For a discussion of the phrase, τὸ πλάτος καὶ μῆκος καὶ ὕψος καὶ βάθος, see T. K. Abbott, The Epistles to

the Ephesians and to the Colossians, ICC, pp. 99-100 and John R. W. Stott, *God's New Society, The Message of Ephesians*, TBST, p. 137. The four words appear to primarily indicate the vastness of God's love which is to be comprehended. However, Stott feels it legitimate to say that the "love of Christ is 'broad' enough to encompass all mankind (especially Jews and Gentiles, the theme of these chapters), 'long' enough to last for eternity, 'deep' enough to reach to the most degraded sinners, and 'high' enough to exalt him to heaven."

[49]Hendriksen, p. 173.

[50]Γνῶναι in Ephesians 3:19 goes beyond the καταλαβέσθαι of 3:18 in respect to the idea of experiential knowledge. Abbott, p. 101.

[51]Hendriksen, p. 117.

[52]A. Skevington Wood, *Ephesians*, in EBC, 12 vols., 11:35.

[53]Murray, 2:113.

[54]Donald Guthrie, *New Testament Theology*, p. 107.

[55]*TDNT*, s.v. "ἔλεος," by Rudolph Bultmann, 2 (1964): 477.

[56]*TNIDNTT*, s.v. "ἔλεος," by H. H. Esser, 2 (1976):594.

[57]Ibid.

[58]Liddell and Scott, s.v. "ἔλεος," p. 536.

[59]*TDNT*, s.v. "ἔλεος," 2 (1964):480.

[60]*TNIDNTT*, s.v. "ἔλεος," 2 (1976):595.

[61]*TDNT*, s.v. "ἔλεος," 2 (1964):480-81.

[62]Ibid., 2 (1964):479. It is also used for חמל six times and five times for נחם.

[63]Ibid., 2 (1964):481.

[64]*TDNT*, s.v. "οἰκτίρω," by Rudolph Bultmann, 5 (1967): 159.

[65]Ibid., 5 (1967):160. [66]Ibid.

[67]Ibid. Οἰκτιρμός may be a slightly stronger term than ἔλεος. Vine, 3:62.

[68]C. E. B. Cranfield, _The Epistle to the Romans_, ICC, 2 vols., 2:587. He understands that both τοὺς πάντας in Romans 11:32 should not be qualified in any sense and yet denies that this teaches universalism. Ibid., 2:588.

[69]Vine, 3:60.

[70]H. C. G. Moule, _Studies in Ephesians_, KPCS, p. 71.

[71]Ibid.

[72]Charles Hodge, _An Exposition of the First Epistle to the Corinthians_, pp. 126-27.

[73]In this verse one sees the principle of Matthew 5:7.

[74]In Paul God is declared to be the Father of the Lord Jesus Christ (Rom. 15:6; 2 Cor. 1:3, 11:31; Eph. 1:3), the Father of believers (Rom. 8:14-16), and Ephesians 3:15 is a possible reference to the universal fatherhood of God.

[75]Philip E. Hughes, _Paul's Second Epistle to the Corinthians_, NIC, p. 61.

[76]Ibid. [77]Ibid., p. 13. [78]Ibid.

[79]Cranfield, 2:596.

[80]John Calvin, _The Epistles of Paul to the Romans and Thessalonians_, CNTC, p. 263.

[81]Ibid.

[82]D. Edmond Hiebert, _Titus and Philemon_, EBC, p. 72.

[83]There appears to be no conclusive evidence that Onesiphorus was dead and this verse sanctions praying for the dead as some have maintained. For a fuller argument against this view see D. Edmond Hiebert, _Second Timothy_, EBC, p. 49.

[84]The ἐν ἐκείνῃ ἡμέρᾳ refers to the day of judgment for the believer (cf. 2 Cor. 5:10). Some see ἔλεος in this verse as merely referring to the consummation of salvation. _Thayer's Greek-English Lexicon of the New Testament_, s.v. "ἔλεος," p. 203. For the OT idea of mercy referring to an eschatological hope see Isaiah 14:1, 49:13, 54:7; Jeremiah 12:15, 33:26; Micah 7:19; and Zechariah 1:16.

[85]R. C. H. Lenski, _The Interpretation of St. Paul's Epistles to the Galatians, Ephesians, and Philippians_, p. 414.

[86]Vine, 3:60. [87]Wood, p. 35.

[88]William G. T. Shedd, *A Critical and Doctrinal Commentary on the Epistle of St. Paul to the Romans*, pp. 288-89.

[89]Vine, 3:62.

[90]James Moffatt, *Grace in the New Testament*, p. 131.

[91]J. A. Robinson, *St. Paul's Epistle to the Ephesians*, p. 221.

[92]*TNIDNTT*, s.v. "χάρις," by H. H. Esser, 2 (1976):116.

[93]Ibid. However, some have argued that χαρις does embrace the concept of חסד. *A Theological Word Book of the Bible*, s.v. "Grace," by N. H. Snaith, p. 101. He says that חסד "stands for God's continual faithfulness to his covenant people, and for his steadfast determination never wholly to let Israel go." Dodd also sees a connection between חסד and χάρις. C. H. Dodd, *The Bible and the Greeks*, pp. 63-64.

[94]*Zondervan Pictorial Encyclopedia of the Bible*, s.v. "Grace," by H. D. McDonald, 2:799.

[95]Ibid.

[96]Richard C. Trench, *Synonyms of the New Testament*, p. 166.

[97]*Zondervan Pictorial Encyclopedia of the Bible*, s.v. "Grace," 2:801.

[98]*TNIDNTT*, s.v. "χάρις," 2 (1976):115.

[99]Donald Guthrie, *New Testament Theology*, p. 106.

[100]Ibid.

[101]*Baker's Dictionary of Theology*, s.v. "Grace," by T. H. L. Parker, p. 258.

[102]Guthrie, p. 106.

[103]Hiebert, *Titus and Philemon*, p. 56.

[104]Homer Kent, *The Pastoral Epistles*, p. 234.

[105]Compare the use of ἐπιφαίνω in Luke 1:79 and Acts 27:20.

[106]*TNIDNTT*, s.v. "χάρις," 2 (1976):115.

[107]Zondervan Pictorial Encyclopedia of the Bible, s.v. "Grace," 2:799.

[108]Charles Hodge, Commentary on the Epistle to the Romans, p. 133.

[109]The verb χαριτόω is used along with the noun χάρις. The only reference to this verb in the NT is Luke 1:28.

[110]Ernest De Witt Burton, A Critical Commentary on the Epistle to the Galatians, ICC, p. 277. "One cannot with intellectual consistency conceive of God as the bookkeeping God of legalism and at the same time the gracious God of the Pauline gospel, who accepts men because of their faith. One cannot live the life of devotion to the keeping of statutes, which legalism calls for, and at the same time a life of faith in Jesus Christ and filial trust in the God of grace. This strong conviction of the incompatibility of the two conceptions, experientially as well as logically, is doubtless grounded in the apostle's own experience."

[111]The optative εἴη should be provided according to Robertson. A. T. Robertson, A Grammar of the Greek New Testament in the Light of Historical Research, p. 396.

[112]R. C. H. Lenski, The Interpretation of St. Paul's Epistle to the Romans, p. 53.

[113]James Moffatt, Grace in the New Testament, p. 141.

[114]Burton, p. 362.

[115]BDB, s.v. "עִם," p. 767. (Cf. Gen. 21:22, 26:3, 31:3, 5; Exod. 3:12; Josh. 1:5; 1 Chron. 11:9; Job 29:5; Ps. 23:4, 46:7, 11; Isa. 7:14; 8:10).

[116]TNIDNTT, s.v. "χάρις," 2 (1976):119.

[117]William Hendriksen, Exposition of 1 & 2 Thessalonians, NTC, p. 42.

[118]Cf. John 1:16.

[119]Charles C. Ryrie, The Grace of God, p. 64. This πᾶσα χάρις notes every kind of divine favor and would include both material and spiritual benefits. Burton, p. 424.

[120]William Hendriksen, Exposition of the Pastoral Epistles, NTC, p. 371.

[121]*Zondervan Pictorial Encyclopedia of the Bible*, s.v. "Grace," 2:801.

[122]Philip E. Hughes, *Commentary on the Second Epistle to the Corinthians*, NIC, p. 332.

[123]William Hendriksen, *Exposition of Ephesians*, NTC, p. 119.

[124]*Baker's Dictionary of Theology*, s.v. "Grace," by T. H. L. Parker, p. 257.

[125]*Zondervan Pictorial Encyclopedia of the Bible*, s.v. "Grace," 2:799.

[126]*Baker's Dictionary of Theology*, s.v. "Grace," p. 258.

[127]Richard C. Trench, *Synonyms of the New Testament*, p. 170.

[128]Ibid., p. 171.

[129]*TDNT*, s.v. "χρηστός," by Konrad Weiss, 9 (1974): 483.

[130]Ibid. [131]Ibid., 19 (1974):484.

[132]*TNIDNTT*, s.v. "χρηστός," by E. Beyreuther, 2 (1976):105.

[133]Ibid. [134]Ibid.

[135]*TDNT*, s.v. "χρηστός," 9 (1974):485.

[136]Ibid., 9 (1974):490. [137]Ibid.

[138]Ibid., 9 (1974):485.

[139]William Barclay, *The Letter to the Romans*, DSBS, pp. 35-36. The only amendment to Barclay's statement is that καλός is a third Greek word which is used for good and in Paul it is a synonym for ἀγαθός. *TNIDNTT*, s.v. "καλός," by E. Beyreuther, 2 (1976):104.

[140]Trench, p. 233.

[141]The word for doing good in Acts 14:17 is ἀγαθοεργέω. If Barclay's distinction holds here, the focus of the root ἀγαθός is on the kind dealings of God who also deals in sterner ways with the nations also.

[142] R. C. H. Lenski, The Interpretation of St. Paul's Epistles to the Galatians, Ephesians, and Philippians, p. 421.

[143] Homer A. Kent, The Pastoral Epistles, p. 420.

[144] Hodge, Romans, p. 48.

[145] D. Edmond Hiebert, Titus and Philemon, EBC, p. 69.

[146] Ibid.

[147] William Hendriksen, Exposition of the Pastoral Epistles, NTC, p. 389.

[148] The πλοῦτος ἐθνῶν of Romans 11:12 is parallel to the χρηστότης θεοῦ of Romans 11:22.

[149] The ideas of severity and goodness are often joined together in the Old Testament (Ps. 125:4-5; Isa. 42:25--43:1, 50:10-11; Nah. 1:6-7).

[150] Trench, p. 199.

[151] TNIDNTT, s.v. "ἀνέχομαι," by V. Falkenroth and C. Brown, 2 (1976):765.

[152] TDNT, s.v. "μακροθυμία," by Johannes Horst, 4 (1967):375.

[153] TNIDNTT, s.v. "μακροθυμία," by V. Falkenroth and C. Brown, 2 (1976):769.

[154] Ibid.

[155] TDNT, s.v. "μακροθυμία," 4 (1967):376.

[156] TNIDNTT, s.v. "μακροθυμία," 2 (1976):769 (cf. Num. 14:18; Ps. 86:15, 103:8; Joel 2:13; Nah. 1:3).

[157] Ibid. [158] Trench, p. 199. [159] Ibid.

[160] Ibid., pp. 198-99.

[161] One might compare Paul's statement in his speech in Athens that God "overlooked the times of ignorance" (Acts 17:30).

[162] TDNT, s.v. "μακροθυμία," 4 (1967):382.

[163] The phrase is τὴν ἅπασαν μακροθυμίαν. D. Edmond Hiebert, First Timothy, EBC, p. 43.

[164]Compare Nahum 1:2-3.

[165]Barclay, New Testament Words, p. 198.

[166]There are also examples in the Old Testament records that cites how this attribute was despised (Jer. 15:15; Jonah 4:2).

[167]TNIDNTT, s.v. "ἀλήθεια," by A. C. Thiselton, 3 (1978):875.

[168]Ibid., 3 (1978):876.

[169]Ibid., 3 (1978):877.

[170]Ibid., 3 (1978):877-82.

[171]TDNT, s.v. "πίστις, πιστός," by Rudolph Bultmann, 6 (1968):175-77.

[172]TWBOT, s.v. "אמנ," by Jack B. Scott, 2 vols., 1:52.

[173]BDB, s.v. "אמנ," pp. 52-53.

[174]Lewis Sperry Chafer, Systematic Theology, 8 vols., vol. 1: Prologomena-Bibliology-Theology Proper, p. 207.

[175]Cranfield, 2:741.

[176]TDNT, s.v. "ἀληθής," by Rudolph Bultmann, 1 (1964): 248.

[177]Cranfield, 1:180.

[178]D. Edmond Hiebert, Titus and Philemon, EBC, p. 23.

[179]Cranfield, 1:143.

[180]Thayer, s.v. "ἀληθινός," p. 27.

[181]Vine, 4:159. [182]Murray, 2:101.

[183]D. Edmond Hiebert, First Timothy, EBC, p. 73.

[184]In all matters of life, the believer can count on the faithfulness and truthfulness of God. As Trench notes, ἀληθής notes that God is true to "the promise of his lips" and ἀληθινός notes that God is true to "the wider promise of his name." Trench, pp. 29-30.

[185]TDNT, s.v. "δικαίος," by Gottlob Schrenk, 2 (1964):182.

[186]Ibid.

[187]TNIDNTT, s.v. "δικαιοσύνη," by H. Seebass, 3 (1978):353.

[188]Liddell and Scott, s.v. "δικαιοσύνη," p. 419.

[189]TNIDNTT, s.v. "δικαιοσύνη," 3 (1978):358.

[190]John Reumann, "The Gospel of the Righteousness of God," Interpretation 20 (October 1966):450.

[191]Christian Friedrich Schmid, Biblical Theology of the New Testament, p. 430.

[192]William Robert Myers, "The Normative Element in Paul's Theologizing: What it is and How it Functions" (Ph.D. dissertation, Emory University, 1971).

[193]Bernhard Weiss, Biblical Theology of the New Testament, 2 vols., 1:317.

[194]Guthrie, p. 99.

[195]Weiss, 1:318.

[196]Cranfield, 1:146.

[197]TDNT, s.v. "προσωποληψία," by Edward Lohse, 6 (1968):780.

[198]Burton, p. 89 (cf. Matt. 22:16; Mark 12:14; Luke 20:21; Jude 16).

[199]TDNT, s.v. "προσωποληψία," 6 (1968): 779 (cf. Gen. 32:20).

[200]This was the standard for the Judges in Israel (Deut.1:17).

[201]Burton, p. 340.

[202]Ibid., p. 341.

[203]Ibid.

[204]Guthrie, p. 101.

[205]Alan Richardson, An Introduction to the Theology of the New Testament, p. 82.

[206]Bernard Weiss, Biblical Theology of the New Testament, 2 vols., 1:317.

[207]Alexander Balmain Bruce, St. Paul's Conception of Christianity, p. 147.

[208]Guthrie, p. 100.

[209]Hiebert, The Thessalonian Epistles, p. 286.

[210]In light of the apparent antithesis with the body, it seems best to take πνεῦμα as a reference to the human spirit. R. L. Godet, Commentary on the Epistle to the Romans, pp. 304-5.

[211]Hiebert, First Timothy, p. 74.

[212]Burton, p. 473. [213]Ibid., p. 274.

[214]Herman N. Ridderbos, The Epistle of Paul to the Churches of Galatia, NIC, pp. 189-90.

[215]Homer A. Kent, The Pastoral Epistles, p. 205.

[216]'Αγιός is used to describe God's Scriptures (Rom. 1:2), His Law (Rom. 7:12), and His calling (2 Tim. 1:9). Likewise the phrase οσιότητι τῆς ἀλημείας occurs in Ephesians 4:24 to describe the new creation of man which is κατὰ θεὸν.

[217]TDNT, s.v. "ὀργή," by Gustav Stahlin, 5 (1967):423.

[218]H. C. G. Moule, Studies in Romans, KPC, p. 58.

[219]Richardson, p. 76.

[220]Liddell and Scott, s.v. "ὀργή," p. 1246.

[221]TNIDNTT, s.v. "ὀργή," by H. C. Hahn, 1 (1975):107.

[222]Ibid., 1 (1975):107-8.

[223]Leon Morris, The Apostolic Preaching of the Cross, p. 131.

[224]Ibid. [225]Ibid.

[226]TNIDNTT, s.v. "ὀργή," 1 (1975):110.

[227]Burton, p. 307.

[228]TNIDNTT, s.v. "θυμός," by H. Schonweiss, 1 (1975): 106.

[229]TDNT, s.v. "θυμός," by Herman Buschel, 3 (1965): 168.

[230]Morris, p. 162. [231]Ibid.

[232]TDNT, s.v. "ὀργή," by Gustav Stahlin, 5 (1967):419.

[233]Murray, 1:66.

[234]TDNT, s.v. "ἐκδικήσις," by Gottlob Schrenk, 2 (1964):446.

[235]TDNT, s.v. "ἀπτομία," by Helmut Koster, 8 (1972): 108.

[236]R. C. H. Lenski, The Interpretation of St. Paul's Epistle to the Romans, p. 90.

[237]Murray, 1:35. [238]Ibid., 1:36.

[239]Cranfield, 1:110. This interpretation ignores the distinction of the "from heaven" in verse 18 and the "in it" of verse 17. H. P. Liddon, Explanatory Analysis of St. Paul's Epistle to the Romans, p. 24.

[240]Lenski, p. 91. [241]Ibid.

[242]F. L. Godet, Commentary on the Epistle to the Romans, p. 101.

[243]Liddon, p. 27. [244]Godet, p. 107.

[245]Ibid. This is also the view of Cranfield, 1:121.

[246]Hodge, p. 44. [247]Cranfield, 2:666.

[248]Murray, 1:171.

[249]TDNT, s.v. "ὀργή," 5 (1967):430.

[250]Wood, p. 35. [251]Cranfield, 1:112.

[252]TDNT, s.v. "μακροθυμία," 4 (1967):382.

[253]J. Benjamin Bedenbaugh, "Paul's Use of 'Wrath of God,'" Lutheran Quarterly 6 (February 1954):156.

[254]Hiebert, The Thessalonian Epistles, p. 291.

[255]Ibid.

[256]Thayer, s.v. "αἰώνιος," p. 21.

[257]William Barclay, The Letter to the Romans, DSBS, pp. 17-19.

[258]*TDNT*, s.v. "ὀργή," 5 (1967):425.

[259]Leon Morris, *The Biblical Doctrine of Judgment*, p. 70.

[260]Guthrie, p. 102.

[261]Willibald Beyschlag, *New Testament Theology or Historical Account of the Teaching of Jesus and of Primitive Christianity According to New Testament Sources*, p. 94.

[262]*TDNT*, s.v. "ὀργή," 5 (1967):425.

[263]Shedd, p. 19. [264]Guthrie, p. 103.

[265]Fernard Prat, *The Theology of St. Paul*, 2 vols., 2:214.

[266]Morris, *The Apostolic Preaching of the Cross*, p. 158.

CHAPTER IV

VOLITIONAL ATTRIBUTES IN PAULINE THEOLOGY

The Sovereignty of God

"The term 'sovereignty' connotes a situation in which a person from his innate dignity, exercises supreme power, with no area of his province outside his jurisdiction."[1] Such was clearly the God of the Apostle Paul. As Williams has stated, "In Paul's view God does not have to 'answer' to man . . . ."[2] He frequently declares this truth in regard to his own salvation (Gal. 1:15-16), in his preaching to others (Acts 17:24-26), in correcting those who object to God's revelation (Rom. 9:19-23), and in the midst of his pastoral instruction (1 Tim. 1:17, 6:15).

The lexical basis

Ryrie cites eight different words which convey Paul's concept of sovereignty--προορίζω, προγινώσκω, ἐκλέγομαι, κλητός, προτίθημι, βουλή, θέλημα, and εὐδοκία.[3] 'Ορίζω, ἐκλεκτός, ἐκλογή, κλῆσις, καλέω, βούλημα, βούλομαι, μέλω, εὐδοκέω, and πρόθεσις could be cited as variations of these terms.

Pauline concepts that relate to sovereignty

Predestination. Προορίζω occurs five times in Paul's writings (Rom. 8:29, 30; 1 Cor. 2:7; Eph. 1:5, 11). It is a very rare and comparatively late Greek word. It occurs from the fourth century B.C. onward and meant to preordain. It is not found in the LXX.[4] Its only other occurrence in the New Testament is in Acts 4:28. The word is a compound word composed of ὁρίζω and πρό. Ὁρίζω means to "determine," "appoint," "fix," or "set."[5] Its other use in Paul's writings is in Romans 1:4, but it does occur in Paul's speech at Athens to denote the fact that the times and boundaries of the nations have been determined by God (Acts 17:26) as well as the truth of the appointment of Christ to be the judge of mankind (Acts 17:31). The prepositional prefix "πρό" means "before,"[6] and the compound means to "decide beforehand." or to "predetermine."[7] As Cremer points out the verb preceded history, but the primary interest in regard to Paul's uses is not on the who but on what is being predestined.[8] Of the five Pauline uses, four refer to God's appointed blessings for believers (Rom. 8:29, 30; Eph. 1:5, 11) and the other to the outworking of God's purpose in respect to the present age (1 Cor. 2:7). The appointed blessings for believers include conformity to the image of Christ, which in Paul involves both an internal (cf. 2 Cor. 3:18) and an external conformity (Phil. 3:21), and adoption into God's family. The pretemporal note of προορίζω is underscored by the πρό τῶν αἰώνων in 1 Corinthians 2:7; and the purpose of this pre-temporal decision is the believer's glory, which is the picture of ultimate conformity to Jesus Christ in that it denotes the believer's glorification.[9] In regard to this concept, Paul's use of προετοιμάζω in Ephesians 2:10 should also be noted.

Paul taught this truth out of his experience with the Lord, who had told him at his conversion what he had been "appointed"[10] to do (Acts 22:10). This "appointment"[11] is spelled out by Ananias as the appointment to know God's will, to see the Righteous One, and to hear an utterance from His mouth (Acts 22:14). As Paul had experienced this truth, he taught it to believers who in their perplexity might know that they can rest in a God who not only provides, but who also predetermines.[12]

Foreknowledge. The key term in Paul's doctrine of foreknowledge is προγινώσκω. In classical Greek it is used with the meaning of "to know or perceive in advance."[13] It occurs only three times in the LXX and always with no Hebrew equivalent. It occurs only five times in the New Testament and both men (Acts 26:5; 2 Pet. 3:17) and God (Rom. 8:29, 11:2; 1 Pet. 1:20) are the subject of this foreknowing. The two uses in Paul are in Romans 8:29 and 11:2. The former refers to God's foreknowing those whom He also predestinated, called, justified, and glorified. The latter refers to God's foreknowledge of Israel. In both cases the concept of

God's election is seen when the force of πρό and γινώσκω, which implies "a knowing that places the knower into a personal relation with the one known,"[14] is considered. Therefore, the use of προγινώσκω in Paul refers to a special relational knowledge that is to be identified with the election of His people.[15]

Election. The key term of this concept is ἐκλέγομαι as well as the corresponding verbal adjective ἐκλεκτός and noun ἐκλογή. In classical Greek ἐκλέγομαι primarily carried the sense of to choose a person or thing.[16] The adjective denoted the person or thing chosen, and the noun denoted the act of choosing.[17] Coenen summarizes the usage of these terms in classical Greek by noting:

> The words of this group are used in various contexts, but wherever they are found, it is evident that certain things common to them all are implied. First, there are several objects from which to choose; secondly, the person making the choice is not tied down by any circumstances which force his hand, but is free to make his own decision. Thirdly, the person making the choice--at least at the moment of choosing--has the person or thing to be chosen at his disposal. Moreover, the act of choosing (and thus the words of this group) includes a judgment by the chooser as to which object he considers to be the most suitable for the fulfillment of his purpose. It is not of vital importance whether it be objective criteria, or subjective feelings and considerations which are paramount in making the decision.[18]

In the LXX, ἐκλέγομαι is almost always used to translate בחר which has roughly the same range of meanings as the Greek verb.[19] The verbal adjective, likewise, most often is used for בחר and its derivatives, and the noun ἐκλογή never occurs in the LXX. Hoehner summarizes the usage of ἐκλέγομαι in the LXX with the following four statements:

a) The choice is made in light of knowing all the options.
b) The choice involves preference. Thus God's choice of us is not cold or calculated but love toward the object he chooses or decides after knowing all the options.
c) In no case was there an example of spurning or a dislike toward the objects not chosen. An example of this is in 1 Sam. 16:8-10 when God chose David and not his brothers after they were considered. The selection of Israel does not mean automatically a rejection of all other nations. The selection of Levi does not mean a rejection of the other tribes (Deut. 18:5).
d) The one chosen has no legal claims on the one who is choosing. God elected Israel because of His choice and love and not because Israel had some legal claim on God.[20]

It is against this background that Paul chooses these terms to develop the concept of God's election.

The time of God's election is most clearly noted by πρὸ καταβολῆς κόσμου in Ephesians 1:4. As Schrenk points out, "This is the one place in the NT where we find ἐκλέγεσθαι with an express accent on eternity."[21] The basis for God's election is His grace (Rom. 11:5) and His purpose (Rom. 9:11). The sphere of God's election is "in Christ" (Eph. 1:4). As Murray says, "The elect were never contemplated apart from Christ."[22] Election in Christ involves the idea of the elect bearing His image and sharing His glory, being saved through His atoning death and resurrection, and the idea that the blessing of election is realized in their union with Christ who is the Last Adam and Head of the new race.[23] The objects of God's election are specifically noted as the elect Jews (Rom. 11:7, cf. Rom. 11:28 and Acts 13:17) and elect individuals of the church (Rom. 8:33; Eph. 1:4; Col. 3:12; 1 Thess. 1:4; Titus 1:1).[24] As the Lord had assured Ananias that Paul was a "chosen instrument" (Acts 9:15), Paul likewise assures believers that they were "the chosen people of God, in contrast with the rest of mankind."[25] Stewart writes:

> What Paul is really trying to do is not to suggest misgivings but to remove them. He is bidding anxious souls reflect that their religion stands in the last resort, not upon their choice of Christ, but upon Christ's choice of them. What a note of ringing confidence, he seems to say, that fact ought to impart to your personal religion.[26]

The end of election in regard to man is his salvation (2 Thess. 2:13), holiness (Eph. 1:4), and glory (Rom. 9:23). The end of election in regard to God is His glory (Eph. 1:6) and the elimination of all improper human boasting (1 Cor. 1:29). The consistent use of the middle voice of ἐκλέγομαι in the New Testament and in Paul's uses of it implies that election is for the benefit of the holy and righteous God. The obligation that election places upon man is to believe the gospel (2 Thess. 2:13), live a life of love and holiness that makes one's election sure (Eph. 1:4; Col. 3:12; 1 Thess. 1:3-4), and rest in the security that God will take care of His elect (Rom. 8:33). Also it was for Paul a motive for evangelism (2 Tim. 2:10).

Nowhere is election explicitly contrasted with a similar decree of damnation.[27] As Ryrie states, "There is preterition, non-election, God passing some by, but never is there inference anywhere that God delights in the destiny of the wicked, that they are driven against their wills, that election nullifies a 'whosoever' gospel, or that an individual can consider himself non-elect and thereby excuse himself in his rejection of Christ."[28] All of God's sovereign dealings with men are declared to be just (Rom. 9:14) and "the viewpoint of Paul's doctrine is always one of amazement that God deals with any man in grace."[29] This amazement is foremost in his own personal experience that God had used His freedom to show mercy (Gal. 1:15-16).

Calling. The verb καλέω and the corresponding κλητός and κλῆσις are ordinary words that acquired a special significance through their baptism into the theological terminology of the New Testament. In both classical and Koine Greek καλέω is used in the sense of invite, summon, or name.[30] In the LXX it is primarily used for קרא, which among other uses does refer to God's calling of Israel (Isa. 41:8-9). Paul uses καλέω twenty-nine times, κλῆσις eight times, and κλητός seven times, and all three terms almost always refer to the divine calling.[31] In contrast to the use of καλέω in the Gospels and Acts where the called are a larger company than the elect (cf. Matt. 22:14), the "called" in Paul's writings designate "those who have not only received the call but also have been won by it."[32] Paul never refers to a rejected call.[33] In Paul's writings, God's call refers to the historical outworking of God's election (Rom. 8:29-30; Gal. 1:15). To this call Paul attributes both His salvation (Gal. 1:15) and His apostleship (Rom. 1:1), and he freely admits his unworthiness of such a calling (1 Cor. 15:9). As Kennedy says, "The supreme wonder of Paul's conversion-crisis was that there God took the initiative."[34]

Paul affirms that all believers have been called by God (cf. Rom. 8:30; Gal. 1:6; 1 Cor. 1:2). The basis for God's calling is not human merit but rather His own purpose and grace (Rom. 8:28; 2 Tim. 1:9), and the means is the gospel message (2 Thess. 2:14). Paul terms this call "holy" (2 Tim. 1:9), "upward" (Phil. 3:14), and irrevocable (Rom. 11:29). It is to result in hope (Eph. 1:18, 4:4), fellowship with Christ and His body (1 Cor. 1:9; Col. 3:15), peace (1 Cor. 7:15), liberty (Gal. 5:13), sanctification (1 Thess. 4:7), and eternal life (1 Tim. 6:12).

Purpose. As Keck puts it, "Paul's understanding of God is telic."[35] The same author writes, "Paul understands history in the light of the intentionality of God."[36] To the same effect Ramsay states that "Paul's thought must always be interpreted as dominated by his conception of the Divine purpose working itself out step by step."[37] Paul uses προτίθημι and the corresponding noun πρόθεσις in relation to the idea of God's purpose. The verb is a compound of πρό, which carries the meaning of in front of or before, and τίμημι, which means to set or place. Thus, the compound means to set before and also developed the meaning of to purpose, resolve, or determine.[38] The noun refers to a setting forth or a presentation and also can mean a plan or purpose.[39] Προτίθημι is found three times in the New Testament and always in Paul's writing. It speaks of God's public setting forth of Christ (Rom. 3:25) and of both Paul's resolve (Rom. 1:13) as well as God's (Eph. 1:9). However, it is Paul's use of πρόθεσις that is especially significant. It occurs twelve times in the New Testament. Four of these twelve is a reference to the showbread (Matt. 12:4; Mark 2:26; Luke 6:4; Heb. 9:2), a use that it commonly had in the LXX. The two other references outside of Paul's writings are a reference to human resolve (Acts 11:23, 27:13). In Paul it takes on a rich theological meaning with five of the six uses referring to God's purpose. God's purpose is said to be immutable (Rom. 9:11), all-inclusive (Eph. 1:11), eternal (Eph. 3:11), and gracious (cf. 2 Tim. 1:9). It is executed in Christ and finds its climax in Him (Eph. 1:9-10, 3:11). It is the basis for God's election (Rom. 9:11), predestination (Eph. 1:11), and calling (Rom. 8:28; 2 Tim. 1:9).

Will. The terms βούλομαι, βουλή, θέλω, θέλημα, εὐδοκία, and εὐδοκέω comprise the Pauline terminology in relationship to the will of God. In classical Greek there appears to have originally been a distinction between βούλομαι and θέλω with the former dealing with a rational and conscious desire and the latter dealing with an impulsive and unconscious desire.[40] While this distinction is disputed and even reversed by some, the important point is that the two words later become virtual synonyms and both could refer to "conscious, decided, and resolute volition."[41] Θέλω was more common in poetry and βούλομαι in prose, and this distinction can be observed in the LXX as well. In Paul's writings θέλω dominates and βούλομαι is used in reference to God's will only once (1 Cor. 12:11). Βουλή "denotes 'deliberation' and 'taking counsel' in all its stages and effects up to 'resolve' and 'decree.'"[42] It is used only twice in Paul's writing where it once refers to the intents of the human heart (1 Cor. 4:5) and once to the counsel and careful deliberation of God (Eph. 1:11). Βούλημα is a later word and described the will "more as a purpose, an intention, a tendency."[43] It is used only three times in the New Testament and the one use in Paul's writings refers to "the purposeful intention of God"[44] (Rom. 9:19). The predominant terms in reference to God's will are θέλω and θέλημα. The former occurs sixty-one times and the latter twenty-four times in Paul's writings.[45] The most important lexical work in relation to these words is a careful analysis of how the terms are employed by Paul. The two other words which contribute to the idea of God's will are εὐδοκέω and εὐκοκία. Εὐδοκέω developed from the impersonal εὖ δοκεῖ τινί τί.[46] In the New Testament it can mean "be well pleased, take delight,"[47] but it can also denote volition in the sense of "choice, resolve, or decree."[48] As a term of volition it emphasizes the emotional element.[49] In relation to God, Paul uses it to refer to timing of his conversion (Gal. 1:15), the deity of the incarnate Son (Col. 1:19), the choice of the means of salvation (1 Cor. 1:21), and God's displeasure of Israel in the wilderness (1 Cor. 10:5). Εὐδοκία has been called a creation of the LXX.[50] It arose out of a need to find a corresponding term for רצון, and of the fifty-six uses of εὐδοκία in the LXX fifty refer to the pleasure or will of God.[51] Paul uses it to refer to God's good pleasure that is expressed in His predestination of the believer to be adopted in His family (Eph. 1:5), the making known of the mystery of His will (Eph. 1:9), and the reason behind His willing and working in the believer's life (Phil. 2:13). In Ephesians 1 the use of εὐδοκία, θέλημα, πρόθεσις, and βουλή is seen (Eph. 1:5, 9, 11). Some hold that the terms are synonyms and view their collective use as strengthening one another and thus more forcefully denoting God's self-determination.[52] It seems to be valid to say that God's good pleasure or εὐδοκία finds expression in His will or θέλημα and that the accomplishment of His will brings Him satisfaction.[53] The deliberate counsel or βουλή that springs forth from His will indicates that "God never acts arbitrarily but with deliberation."[54] The πρόθεσις "indicates the 'purpose' of this plan or the 'plan itself' from the point of view of what it 'aims' to accomplish; God's 'design.'"[55]

An examination of the relevant passages in Paul's

writings shows that these terms convey the idea of a sovereign will of God. The apostle noted that it is certain of accomplishment (Rom. 9:19), all-inclusive (Eph. 1:11), the expression of God's kind intention (Eph. 1:5), and guided by God's attributes (cf. Rom. 9:22). He also noted that God has ordained means such as prayer in the accomplishment of this sovereign will (Rom. 15:32). While Satan and his subjects are said to have a will (2 Tim. 2:26), neither of these are viewed as sovereign or as able to overthrow God's rule (cf. Rom. 9:16). Some of the actions of God that are specifically said to be in accordance with His sovereign will are the giving of spiritual gifts (1 Cor. 12:11), the exact placement of each member of the body of Christ (1 Cor. 12:18), the timing of God's revelation (Eph. 1:9; Col. 1:27), the death of Christ and the subsequent deliverance of the believer from the present evil age (Gal. 1:4), the sovereign working of God in the believer's life (Phil. 2:13), the giving of the resurrected body (1 Cor. 15:38), and Paul's apostleship (1 Cor. 1:1; 2 Cor. 1:1; Eph. 1:1; Col. 1:1; 2 Tim. 1:1). Paul respected this sovereign will and subjected his plans to it (Rom. 1:10; 1 Cor. 4:19) and likewise urged others to submit their thinking to it (Rom. 9:16-23). As Ramsay has said in regard to the sovereign will in Paul:

> To him the process of human affairs was the gradual evolution of the Divine will within those conditions of time and space that hedge men in. . . . That apparently evil seems to triumph is due to our taking too narrow a view: take a wider view, fetch a wider compass, and you

> perceive that the Divine will is triumphant in its own way and at its own proper time.[56]

In Paul's writings, "the will of God is the soul of history."[57]

In Paul's writings there is also a clear teaching on God's revealed will in His word. The common distinction of God's decretive or providential will and His preceptive or revealed will does flow out of Paul's discussion of the will of God. The preceptive or revealed will of God is expressed in the Scriptures (Rom. 2:18). It can be understood (Eph. 5:17), obeyed (Eph. 6:6), and approved (Rom. 12:2). Paul prayed that the believers at Colossae would be filled or controlled by an experiential knowledge of God's revealed will (Col. 1:11), and the prayer of Epaphras for these believers is that they would stand firm and be fully assured in the will of God (Col. 4:12). The sanctification of the believer as well as continual rejoicing, prayer, and thanksgiving are specifically declared to be the will of God (1 Thess. 4:3, 5:18).[58] The believer is to live within the guidelines of God's revealed will and also submit himself to God's providential and sovereign will (1 Cor. 4:19).[59] The preceptive will of God may be disobeyed but the providential will of God is certain of ultimate accomplishment.[60]

Kingdom. While the purpose of this study is not to deal exhaustively with Paul's view of the kingdom, it should be noted that the very concept of a kingdom does imply sovereignty. The kingdom in Paul's writings can be looked at in at least three ways. First, there is the eternal kingdom of God in which He providentially rules over His creation (cf. Col. 1:16-17). In this sense God is the "King of the ages" (1 Tim. 1:17), the "only Sovereign, King of kings, and Lord of lords" (1 Tim. 6:15), and the One Who appoints all authority (Rom. 13:1, cf. Col. 2:10). Secondly, believers are said to have been transferred from the kingdom of darkness into the kingdom of Christ (Col. 1:13). Thirdly, believers also await the prospect of a future kingdom and the judgment of all rebellion (2 Tim. 4:1; 1 Cor. 15:24; cf. Phil. 2:10).

The foundational nature of sovereignty in Paul's writings

The centrality of this truth in all of Paul's writings is well summarized by Ryrie when he comments in particular on Paul's eschatology:

> As all of Paul's theology, his eschatology is theocentric. The entire Pauline system seems to be rooted and grounded in the apostle's conception of God. The future for the church is in the hands of her Sovereign Head, who will return personally to take her to be with Himself. That Israel will have a future is guaranteed by the 'gifts and calling of God [which are] without repentance.' (Rom. 11:29). The world will be judged because 'it is a righteous thing with God to recompense tribulation to them that trouble you' (II Thess. 1:6); and the assurance of resurrection rests on the power of God who gives the body and who according to His mighty power raised Jesus from the dead (1 Cor. 15:38; Eph. 1:19-20). In every area of eschatology Paul's thought reflects his basic conception of the sovereign God. The consummation of all things depends on this God who in the forging of

> His majestic plan made no miscalculation and who in the execution of it leaves no gaps or imperfections.[61]

On every page of Paul's writings one sees the imprints of his view of God's sovereignty. Of course, he sees this from the viewpoint of his own conversion and life. In regard to his conversion Keck writes:

> Implicit in his conversion is the radical freedom of God vis-à-vis Paul's life, for his conversion implied that God was not bound in the way Paul was thinking of God or relating to him. Rather, God intervened in his life despite Paul. The logic of this experience implies that a God who is not free to do this cannot do anything decisive about the human situation; conversely, a God who has done this is disclosed as a radically free sovereign committed to setting things right.[62]

In regard to Paul's life Barclay notes, "Paul sees God's hand in his own spiritual pilgrimage. He saw his life as something planned and designed by God."[63] The same author also states, "He did not see God only in the great events and the crucial moments on which his life had hinged. He saw God in the life of everyday."[64] As Paul teaches this doctrine he does not attempt to satisfy all speculative curiosity but he writes with the desire of a pastor to produce a sense of humility, confidence, and courage in his fellow believers.

The Power of God

The primary words that are used in relation to the power of God are δύναμις, δύναμαι, δυνατός, δυναμόω, δυνάστης, δυνατέω, ἐνέργεια, ἐνεργέω, ἐνέργημα, ἐνεργής, ἱκανός, ἱκανότης, ἱκανόω, ἰσχύς, ἰσχυρός, κράτος, κτίζω, κτίσις, σημεῖον, and τέρας. The "words deriving from the stem δύνα- all have the basic meaning of 'being able.'"[65] Δύναμις suggests "the inherent capacity of someone or something to carry something out."[66] It can also denote the expression of this capacity.[67] Therefore, it can denote both "power capable of action" and "power in action."[68] In the latter sense, it is used as a New Testament word for miracle (2 Cor. 12:12; Gal. 3:5). As a miracle δύναμις draws attention to the exhibition of the divine power, σημεῖον draws attention to what the miracle signified, and τέρας draws attention to the "wonderful portent or prodigy."[69] Δύναμαι means "to be strong enough" or "to be able to."[70] The other meanings of the words in this group are as follows: δυνατός, "powerful, strong, mighty, able"; δυναμόω, "strengthen"; δυνάστης, "a ruler, sovereign"; δυνατέω, "be strong, able, strong enough."[71] 'Ενέργεια, ἐνεργέω, ἐνέργημα, and ἐνεργής are "always used to describe the action of some power which is beyond the power of man and the power of this world."[72] In the New Testament they are used almost exclusively to denote the work of either demonic powers or far more frequently the power of God. Barclay writes:

> These words have the meaning of vitality as opposed to deadness, activity as opposed to idleness, efficiency as opposed to uselessness, effective activity as opposed to ineffectiveness. All these ideas will light up the conception of the divine activity of God.[73]

'Ενέργεια is a noun that carries the meaning of activity or operation. It is not used for simply action but effective action that "issues in the desired and proposed result."[74] It is not simply energy but "focused, purposeful, meaningful, effective, energetic action."[75] It occurs nine times in the New Testament and always in Paul's writings. Ἐνεργέω means "to be in action" or "to operate" and also carries the idea of effectiveness.[76] It is used in the New Testament nineteen times, and all but three of these uses are in Paul's writings. Ἐνέργημα refers to an activity or operation which was actively done as opposed to something that was merely endured.[77] It occurs twice in the New Testament and both times it is in Paul's writings where he refers to the effects of spiritual gifts (1 Cor. 12:6, 10). Ἐνεργής carries the idea of powerful and effective action.[78] It occurs three times in the New Testament and twice in Paul's writings. Ἱκανός has the basic sense of "adequate, sufficient, enough, or large enough."[79] Paul employs it in declaring his own insufficiency in and of himself (1 Cor. 15:9; 2 Cor. 2:16, 3:5). Ἱκανότης denotes "sufficiency," "competency," or "competency to do a thing."[80] Its only occurrence denotes the sufficiency of God which Paul leaned on for his own sufficiency (2 Cor. 3:5). Ἱκανόω means to "make sufficient" or "to qualify"[81] and both New Testament uses are in Paul's writings (2 Cor. 3:6; Col. 1:12). "The word group ἰσχύ- has the meaning 'to be able,' 'to be capable,' 'capacity,' 'power,' strength.'"[82] It is therefore closely related to the δύνα- word group but places slightly more emphasis on the actual power that is implied in the ability or capacity, while the other word group places the emphasis on the inherent ability or capacity.[83] Ἰσχύς denotes "strength, power, or might"[84] and its three uses in Paul refer to God's power (Eph. 1:19, 6:10; 2 Thess. 1:9). Ἰσχυρός means "strong, powerful, mighty,"[85] and in 1 Corinthians 1:25 the comparative form is used to denote the superiority of God's power over man's. Κράτος places the attention on the presence and significance of power, might, and strength.[86] In the New Testament it is always used of either demonic power or God's power. The four references in Paul denote God's power (Eph. 1:19, 6:10; Col. 1:11; 1 Tim. 6:16). Of course Paul's use of κτίζω and κτίσις also draws attention to God's power. The discussion that follows is an attempt to exhibit the Pauline teaching that flows from the use of these words in his revelation.

Supremacy of God's power

The concept of sovereignty deals with God's supreme authority and the necessary correlation is His supreme power. Paul's writings speak of the power of sin which is at work in the members of the body (Rom. 7:5), of the mystery of lawlessness that is at work (2 Thess. 2:7), and of the working of demonic power in the sons of disobedience (Eph. 2:2, cf. 6:12); but the apostle always upholds the supremacy of God's power in such a way that assures his readers that evil will never be able to ultimately triumph over God (1 Cor. 15:24; Phil. 2:10, 3:21).[87] The supremacy of God's power is seen in the fact that it is eternal and thus part of His very essence (Rom. 1:20). All other creatures have only the power that the God, who has created all things (Eph. 3:9), has assigned. The supremacy of God's power is also seen in such titles as παντοκράτωρ (2 Cor. 6:18) and δυνάστης (1 Tim. 6:15).[88] It is because of the supremacy of God's power that the apostle exclaims "If God is for us, who can be against us" (Rom. 8:31).

Power is guided by God's attributes

It is clear in Paul's revelation that this power is not an uncontrolled force, but it is consistent with His attributes. It is for this reason that he writes that God cannot lie (Titus 1:2) and that God cannot deny Himself (2 Tim. 2:13).

Power gives activity to God's attributes

In Paul the attributes of God are not static qualities. They are not only truths about God, but they also have been displayed through His power. For this reason, the help that God provides through His mercy and grace is associated with His power (cf. 2 Cor. 9:8, 12:9; 2 Tim. 2:1).

Contrasted with man's weakness

A distinct emphasis in the revelation of this attribute is the contrast between man's inability and God's ability. The inability of man in the flesh (Rom. 8:7, 8) and the natural man (1 Cor. 2:14) is in contrast with the God "who is able" (Rom. 4:21, 14:4, 16:25; Eph. 3:20; 2 Tim. 1:12). Likewise, in the case of the believer the contrast is between his inadequacy in and of himself and God's adequacy (2 Cor. 2:16, 3:5-6). It is for this reason that Paul speaks of God displaying His power in his weakness (2 Cor. 12:9-10; cf. 2 Cor. 4:7, 13:9). Indeed, "the weakness of God is stronger than men" (1 Cor. 1:25).

In relation to Paul's life

Paul attributed his conversion and apostleship to the working of God's power (Eph. 3:7) as well as the results of his ministry that flowed from God's working (Gal. 2:8). The very open doors for service are attributed to God's working (1 Cor. 16:9). His preaching was said to be a demonstration of God's power and he desired that this power be the resting place of men's faith (1 Cor. 2:4-5; cf. 2 Cor. 6:7, 13:4; 1 Thess. 1:5). As an apostle he displayed the power of God through the working of miracles which attested to the authenticity of his ministry and message (Rom. 15:19; 2 Cor. 12:12; Gal. 3:5). The fact that he depended upon the power of God is seen in his referring to the weapons of his warfare as divinely powerful (2 Cor. 10:4) and to the fact that his labor and his striving was according to God's power which was at work in him (Col. 1:29). He was unquestionably personally acquainted with the power of God. As Forster said, "There are two foci around which St. Paul's thinking about power revolve: one was his conviction that Jesus was risen, the other his own personal experiences as a missionary."[89]

Display of God's power

Creation. God's eternal power is said to have been manifested to all men since the creation of the world (Rom. 1:20). God is specifically declared to be the Creator (Rom. 1:25), and a sample of Paul's preaching ministry includes this fact (Acts 17:24). This creative work extends to all things according to Ephesians 3:9, and the specific creation of man and woman is cited in 1 Corinthians 11:9.

However, the creation of the world is not the only creative act of God that Paul discusses. He declares the believer to be a new creation of God (2 Cor. 5:17; Gal. 6:15). The believer is said to have been created in Christ Jesus (Eph. 2:10) and in righteousness and holiness (Eph. 4:24). Likewise, the church is specifically said to be a creation of God (Eph. 2:15).

Providence. The God who created this world is also cited as the One who providentially sustains it (Col. 1:17; cf. Acts 14:17). It displays His power as He "works" all things after the counsel of His will (Eph. 1:11). In a special way the believer is subject to God's providential care. Guthrie writes:

> Although it is maintained that providence affects all men, some distinctions are made over God's special concern for those who believe in him, mainly in the realm

of spiritual blessing. According to Romans 8:28 God excercises control over all aspects of the lives of believers, which arises from his special concern as Father for his children.[90]

Miracles. God's power has been displayed in miracles. Paul refers to the miracles in his ministry as the "signs of an apostle" (2 Cor. 12:12; cf. Rom. 15:19; Gal. 3:5). He, likewise, refers to the gift of miracles (1 Cor. 12:10, 28, 29). God's display of miracles in Egypt is also cited by Paul as a demonstration of His power (Rom. 9:17).

Gospel. The gospel is said to be the power of God for salvation to everyone who believes (Rom. 1:16). The point is that where there is faith in the gospel, "the omnipotence of God is operative unto salvation."[91] In a similar vein he declared "the word of the cross" and the preaching of "Christ crucified" to be the power of God (1 Cor. 1:18, 23-24).

Judgment. The demonstration of God's wrath is associated with God's making known His power (Rom. 9:22). The future display of God's wrath will be the time that all will recognize the Almighty for who He is (cf. 1 Cor. 15:24; Phil. 2:10). It is noteworthy that the picture of eternal destruction in Paul is viewed as a separation from "the glory of His power" (2 Thess. 1:9).[92]

Resurrection of Christ. The resurrection of Christ was a grand display of the power of God (Rom. 1:4; 1 Cor.

6:14; 2 Cor. 13:4; Eph. 1:19-20). It is for this reason that Paul writes of the "power of the resurrection" (Phil. 3:10). This is the display of God's power over the sin and death that entered the world through the rebellion of man (cf. Rom. 5:12).

Ascension of Christ. God's power was displayed not only in the raising of Christ from the dead but also in His being seated at God's right hand (Eph. 1:19-21; cf. Col. 2:10). This is the display of God's power over the demonic world (Eph. 1:21, 6:12; cf. Col. 2:15).

Bodily resurrection of the believer. The same power that raised Christ from the dead will also be displayed in the resurrection of the believer (1 Cor. 6:14, 15:43). The transformation of the present unredeemed body (cf. Rom. 8:23) to the glorious resurrected body will be accomplished by the "exertion of His power" (Phil. 3:21).

Within the church. Ἐνέργεια is used in Ephesians 4:16 to denote the divine power that works through each part of the body of Christ so as to create growth in the body. This is similar to the use of ἐνεργέω and ἐνέργημα in 1 Corinthians 12:6 and the use of the latter in 1 Corinthians 12:10. These words denote the working of God in the church through the spiritual gifts that He gives.

In the believer. Paul taught that the kingdom of God consisted in power (1 Cor. 4:20), and that this royal power was available to the believer. The relation of this power to Paul's life and ministry has already been discussed. The apostle, who knew the reality of this power in his own life (Col. 1:29) and longed to experience it in its fullest measure (Phil. 3:10), prayed for other believers that they also would be enlightened to know that God's power was available to them (Eph. 1:15-23). While he taught that there would be some in the last days who would deny this power (2 Tim. 3:5), it was to be the object of faith for the true believer (1 Cor. 2:5; Col. 2:12). Realizing the power of sin and satanic forces, the believer is to draw upon the Lord's strength as he walks by the Spirit (Gal. 5:16; Eph. 6:10-12). In light of the truth that God indwells the believer (Rom. 8:9; 1 Cor. 6:19; Gal. 2:20), "this power was not an external possession which could be mechanically transferred (cf. Acts 8:19ff.), but a living presence in the believer (cf. Rom. 15:13; 2 Cor. 13:3ff.)."[93] The Lord is said to be the One who is able to make the believer stand (Rom. 14:4), to strengthen him so that he can patiently endure suffering (2 Cor. 1:6; Col. 1:11; 2 Tim. 1:8), and to fulfill every desire for goodness and work of faith (2 Thess. 1:11). It is this power that is at work in the believer's life providing the desire and the power to do God's will (Phil. 2:13). As Barclay has written:

> . . . to Paul God was a supplying God. This God, who creates men, and who directed their lives, did not leave them to carry out His commandments unaided and to go upon His tasks unassisted. With the need came the power; with the task came the ability to do it.[94]

It is this power that is at work in the believer's life that is able to do exceedingly abundantly beyond all that he can ask or think (Eph. 3:20). "To Paul a Christian was a man who had the continual support of God."[95]

Notes

[1]ZPBE, s.v. "Sovereignty of God," by H. B. Kuhn, 5:498.

[2]Sam K. Williams, "The 'Righteousness of God' in Romans," Journal of Biblical Literature 99 (June 1980):290.

[3]Charles Caldwell Ryrie, Biblical Theology of the New Testament, pp. 169-70.

[4]TNIDNTT, s.v. "προορίζω," by P. Jacobs and H. Krienke, 1 (1975):695.

[5]BAG, 4th rev. ed., s.v. "ὁρίζω," p. 584.

[6]Ibid., s.v. "πρό," p. 708.

[7]Thayer, s.v. "προορίζω," p. 541.

[8]Hermann Cremer, Biblico-Theological Lexicon of New Testament Greek, p. 462.

[9]R. C. H. Lenski, The Interpretation of St. Paul's First and Second Epistles to the Corinthians, p. 98.

[10]Τάσσω is used in Acts 22:10 which carries the idea of "fix, determine, or appoint." BAG, 4th rev. ed., s.v. "τάσσω," p. 813.

[11]Προχειρίζομαι is used in Acts 22:14 which means to "choose for oneself, select, appoint." BAG, 4th rev. ed., s.v. "προχειρίζω," p. 731.

[12]A Theological Word Book of the Bible, s.v. "Determinate," by J. K. S. Reid, p. 68.

[13]TNIDNTT, s.v. "προγινώσκω," by R. Jacobs and H. Krienke, 1 (1975):692.

[14]R. C. H. Lenski, The Interpretation of St. Paul's Epistle to the Romans, p. 557. Also Cremer, p. 161 (cf. Hos. 13:5; Amos 3:2; 1 Cor. 8:3; Gal. 4:9; 2 Tim. 2:19).

[15]TDNT, s.v. "προγινώσκω," by Rudolph Bultmann, 1 (1964):715. For a further support of this view of foreknowledge, see John Murray, The Epistle to the Romans, NIC,

2 vols., 7:315-18 and ZPBE, s.v. "Foreknow, foreknowledge," by John Murray, 2:590-93.

[16]TNIDNTT, s.v. "ἐκλέγομαι," by L. Coenen, 1 (1975): 536.

[17]It should be noted that ἐκλέγομαι can carry the secondary sense of "to levy a tax or tribute" and "to declare." Harry Liddell and George Scott, A Greek-English Lexicon, s.v. "ἐκλέγομαι," p. 511. However, these uses are not germane to the Pauline usage of the term.

[18]TNIDNTT, s.v. "ἐκλέγομαι," 1 (1975):536.

[19]Ibid., 1 (1975):537.

[20]Harold W. Hoehner, class notes in 906 Principles of Exegesis, Dallas Theological Seminary, Spring 1976.

[21]TDNT, s.v. "ἐκλέγομαι," by Gottlob Schrenk, 4 (1967):175. The ἀπ ἀρχῆς of 2 Thessalonians 2:13 might also link God's choosing (εἵλατο) to eternity past. The alternate reading ἀπαρχὴν is likewise well-attested but it does not suit the context as well and Paul never uses the idea of first-fruits in connection with election. Second Timothy 1:9 also makes a contribution to this idea.

[22]ZPBE, s.v. "Elect, election," by John Murray, 2:273.

[23]NBD, s.v. "Election," by J. I. Packer, p. 360.

[24]Paul also refers to elect angels (1 Tim. 5:21).

[25]NBD, s.v. "Election," p. 359. The use of in Romans 16:13 may be an indication of Paul ascribing this title to an individual as interpreted by C. E. B. Cranfield, A Critical and Exegetical Commentary on the Epistle to the Romans, 2 vols., 2:794. The alternate view is to interpret the term as meaning "choice" in the sense of outstanding. Murray, 2:231.

[26]James S. Stewart, A Man in Christ: The Vital Parts of St. Paul's Religion, p. 144.

[27]TDNT, s.v. "ἐκλέγομαι," 4 (1967):175.

[28]Ryrie, pp. 173-74. [29]Ibid., p. 171.

[30]TNIDNTT, s.v. "καλέω," by L. Coenen, 1 (1975):271. James Hope Milligan and George Milligan, The Vocabulary of the Greek Testament, p. 318.

[31]*TNIDNTT*, s.v. "καλέω," 1 (1975):275.

[32]Lenski, *Romans*, p. 555.

[33]Ernest De Witt Burton, *A Critical and Exegetical Commentary on the Epistle to the Galatians*, ICC, p. 20.

[34]H. A. A. Kennedy, *The Theology of the Epistles*, p. 133.

[35]Leander E. Keck, *Paul and His Letters*, Proclamation Commentaries, p. 66.

[36]Ibid., p. 67.

[37]W. M. Ramsay, *The Teaching of Paul in Terms of the Present Day*, p. 91.

[38]*TNIDNTT*, s.v. "προτίθημι," by P. Jacobs and H. Krienke, 1 (1975):696.

[39]BAG, 4th rev. ed., s.v. "πρόθεσις," p. 713.

[40]*TDNT*, s.v. "βούλομαι," by Gottlob Schrenk, 1 (1964): 629.

[41]Ibid., 1 (1964):630.

[42]*TDNT*, s.v. "βουλή," by Gottlob Schrenk, 1 (1964): 633.

[43]*TNIDNTT*, s.v. "βούλομαι," by D. Muller, 3 (1978): 1015.

[44]*TDNT*, s.v. "βούλημα," by Gottlob Schrenk, 1 (1964): 637.

[45]*TNIDNTT*, s.v. "μέλω," by D. Muller, 3 (1978):1019.

[46]*TDNT*, s.v. "εὐδοκέω," by Gottlob Schrenk, 2 (1964): 738.

[47]BAG, 4th rev. ed., s.v. "εὐδοκέω," p. 319.

[48]*TDNT*, s.v. "εὐδεκέω," 2 (1964):741.

[49]Ibid., 2 (1964):739.

[50]*TDNT*, s.v. "εὐδοκία," by Gottlob Schrenk, 2 (1964): 742.

[51]Ibid., 2 (1964):742-43.

[52]Ibid., 2 (1964):747.

[53]A. Skevington Wood, Ephesians, TEBC, 12 vols., 11:25.

[54]William Hendriksen, Exposition of Ephesians, NTC, p. 88.

[55]Ibid. [56]Ramsay, p. 91. [57]Ibid.

[58]The τοῦτο of 1 Thessalonians 5:18 appears to also include the commands of 1 Thessalonians 5:16-17 as well as 5:18. D. Edmond Hiebert, The Thessalonian Epistles, p. 242.

[59]For an example of the interaction of these two in the apostle's prayer life see Murray, 1:21. In Paul there is a relative freedom within the revealed will of God which would include all the eternal principles and commandments of Scripture (cf. 1 Cor. 7:36, 39).

[60]First Timothy 2:4 expresses God's desire that all men be saved. Unless one limits the all to the elect, this is an example of God's preceptive will where His desire is not identified with His decree.

[61]Ryrie, p. 220. [62]Keck, p. 66.

[63]William Barclay, The Mind of St. Paul, p. 37.

[64]Ibid., p. 38.

[65]TDNT, s.v. "δύναμαι," by Walter Grundmann, 2 (1964):284.

[66]TNIDNTT, s.v. "δύναμις," by O. Betz, 2 (1976):601.

[67]Ibid.

[68]Hermann Cremer, Biblico-Theological Lexicon of New Testament Greek, p. 218.

[69]George Ricker Berry, A Dictionary of New Testament Greek Synonyms, p. 37.

[70]TNIDNTT, s.v. "δύναμις," 2 (1976):601.

[71]Ibid.

[72]William Barclay, New Testament Words, p. 77

[73]Ibid., pp. 78-79. [74]Ibid., p. 79.

[75]Ibid., p. 80. [76]Ibid. [77]Ibid.

[78]Ibid., p. 81.

[79]TDNT, s.v. "ἱκανός," by Karl Rengstorf, 3 (1965): 293.

[80]Thayer, s.v. "ἱκανότης," p. 300.

[81]BAG, 4th rev. ed., s.v. "ἱκανόω," p. 375.

[82]TDNT, s.v. "ἰσχύω," by Walter Grundmann, 3 (1965): 397.

[83]Ibid.

[84]TNIDNTT, s.v. "ἰσχύω," by G. Braumann, 3 (1978): 712.

[85]Ibid.

[86]TDNT, s.v. "κράτος," by Wilhelm Michaelis, 3 (1965):905.

[87]The believer also pictured as triumphant over the powers of sin and Satan (Gal. 5:16; Eph. 6:10-13) in light of his position in Christ (Eph. 1:21-22, 2:4).

[88]The meaning of these terms has already been briefly referred to under the lexical basis.

[89]A. Haire Forster, "The Meaning of Power for St. Paul," Anglican Theological Review 32 (1950):178.

[90]Donald Guthrie, New Testament Theology, p. 80.

[91]Murray, 1:28.

[92]This refers to the power that has been "manifested in the salvation of the saints." William Hendriksen, Exposition of I and II Thessalonians, NTC, p. 161.

[93]Baker's Dictionary of Theology, s.v. "Power, powers," by Donald Guthrie, p. 411.

[94]William Barclay, The Mind of St. Paul, p. 38.

[95]Ibid., p. 39.

CHAPTER V

CONSTITUTIONAL ATTRIBUTES IN PAULINE THEOLOGY

The Eternality of God

The lexical basis

The words that are employed in connection with this attribute are ἀίδιος, αἰών, and αἰώνιος. ʼΑίδιος carries the meaning of eternal, everlasting, and continual.[1] In the LXX it is found only in the Apocrypha (Wi 7:26; IV Ma 10:15). It occurs only twice in the New Testament (Rom. 1:20; Jude 6). Cremer notes its relation to the synonym αἰώνιος when he states that it specifically excludes the idea of interruption and "lays stress upon permanence and unchangeableness, especially with reference to the past or the present."[2] In classical Greek αἰών could refer to a lifetime, an indefinitely long time, and in philosophical language to eternity.[3] In the LXX it is used to translate some nine Hebrew words with עולם being by far the most frequent. There are a number of examples where the given context links its meaning to that of eternity.[4] It occurs over one hundred times in the New Testament and nineteen times in Paul.[5] Αἰών views the world under the aspect of time while κόσμος views the world under the aspect of space.[6] The indefinitely long period of time that αἰών denotes may refer to the unbroken age of eternity.[7] This eternal age may have a retrospective look into the past as in 1 Corinthians 2:7, Ephesians 3:9, and Colossians 1:26 where "the meaning verges on pre-temporal eternity."[8] It more frequently points to the endless future. While αἰών itself may carry "the full significance of eternity,"[9] this idea is strengthened by the phrase εἰς τὸν αἰῶνα (2 Cor. 9:9) and especially by the plural in the phrases εἰς τοὺς αἰῶνας (Rom. 1:25, 11:36, 16:27; 2 Cor. 11:31) and εἰς τοὺς αἰῶνας τῶν αἰώνων (Gal. 1:5; Phil. 4:20; 1 Tim. 1:17; 2 Tim. 4:18; cf. Eph. 3:21). The plural "presupposes knowledge of a plurality of αἰῶνες, of ages and periods of time whose infinite series constitutes eternity."[10] The adjective αἰώνιος carried the meaning of an indefinite period of time, perpetual, or eternal in classical Greek.[11] In the LXX it is used only for עולם and its cognates. In Koine Greek it became a standing adjective to describe the Emperor's power in that the royal power of Rome was declared to be perpetual and to last forever.[12] In the New Testament αἰώνιος is the "word of the eternal order as contrasted with the order of this world; it is a word of deity as contrasted with humanity; essentially it is a word which can be properly applied to no one other than God."[13] It is used most often to refer to eternal life which is the life that belongs to God.[14] In Paul it is often used in this way (Rom. 2:7, 5:21, 6:23; Gal. 6:8; 1 Tim. 1:16, 6:12, 19; Titus 1:2, 3:7). Related are the references to eternal comfort (2 Thess. 2:16) and eternal glory (2 Tim. 2:10). It also is used to refer to eternal destruction (2 Thess. 1:9), of the past ages (Rom. 16:25; 2 Tim. 1:9; Titus 1:2), the eternal God (Rom. 16:26), the rewards that await the suffering believer (2 Cor. 4:17-18), and the resurrected body (2 Cor. 5:1). Notable is the reference in 2 Corinthians 4:1 where it is contrasted to πρόσκαιρα which denotes that which is temporal. Αἰώνιος can refer to that which is without beginning or end, that which is without a beginning, and that which is without an end.[15] Sasse notes that the concept of eternity is weakened by the phrase χρόνοι αἰώνιοι (Rom. 16:25; 2 Tim. 1:9; Titus 1:2).[16] It is consistent, however, with the language of the New Testament which speaks of eternity in the categories of time.[17] The only occurrence of the adjective without a corresponding noun is in Philemon 15.[18]

Treatment of this attribute in Paul's writings

In doxologies. The one occasion that αἰώνιος is specifically attributed to God is in Romans 16:26. The context is a closing doxology, and in Paul's writing the concept of eternity is most frequently connected with the eternal praise that is ascribed to God (Rom. 1:25, 11:36, 16:27; 2 Cor. 11:31; Gal. 1:5; Eph. 3:21; Phil. 4:20; 1 Tim. 1:17, 2 Tim. 4:18). This praise is found in contexts where God is seen as Creator (Rom. 1:25), omniscient (2 Cor. 11:31), wise (Rom.

11:36, 16:27), Redeemer (Gal. 1:5), powerfully at work in the believer's life (Eph. 3:21), able to meet the believer's needs (Phil. 4:20), the Eternal King (1 Tim. 1:18) and able to deliver His children from all evil (2 Tim. 4:18).

In relation to His purpose. The eternal God is declared to be the "King of the ages" in 1 Timothy 1:17. As Liddon says, "The ages in the aggregate suggest eternity."[19] As the "King of the ages" He is said to have a "purpose of the ages" or an eternal purpose (Eph. 3:11). This eternal purpose is related to history in that it was carried out in Christ (Eph. 3:11) who was sent in the fullness of time (Gal. 4:4) and who died at the right time (Rom. 5:6). Also the man of lawlessness will come in his appointed time (2 Thess. 2:6) which is one of the events that God will use to prepare the way for the administration of the fullness of time (Eph. 1:10). The point that Paul clearly makes is that the eternal God is working out His eternal purpose in history.

In relation to other attributes. The attribute of eternality in relation to God is of course also a truth of all of His attributes. For example, God's power is specifically declared to be eternal in Romans 1:20. Paul's quote of Psalm 112:9 in 2 Corinthians 9:9 declares God's righteousness to be forever. The riches of God's grace which were conceived from eternity (2 Tim. 1:9) are said to be on display for all eternity (Eph. 2:7). His eternal purpose is a product of His manifold wisdom (Eph. 3:10-11). The eternal nature of His punishment (2 Thess. 1:9) is a reflection of His holy and eternal reaction to unrighteousness. The gift of eternal life is a reflection of His own eternal life (Rom. 6:23).

In relation to Paul's life. It is this attribute that brought particular comfort to Paul as he viewed his afflictions and sufferings as temporary (2 Cor. 4:17-18; cf. Rom. 8:18). Likewise, it affected his total view of his life in this world. As one who had been delivered out of this present evil age (Gal. 1:4) and who was a citizen of heaven (Phil. 3:20), his concern for this life was to walk wisely by making full use of every God-given opportunity (Eph. 5:16). He focused his attentions and pursuits on the eternal (2 Cor. 4:18; Col. 3:1-2; cf. 1 Tim. 6:7) as he sought to finish the task that God had given him to accomplish (2 Tim. 4:7; cf. Acts 20:24; Phil. 3:12).

The Immortality of God

The lexical basis

Ἀθανασία is primarily a literary term in classical Greek and carries the meaning of immortality.[20] It is a quality proper to the gods but whether it is true of the human soul is a matter of dispute.[21] It is found only in the LXX apogrypha and is used to denote the expected state of the righteous (Wis. 3:4, 15:3; 4 Macc. 14:5).[22] Moulton and Milligan demonstrate that this term had the connotation of freedom from death.[23] It is found only three times in the New Testament, and all three are in Paul's writings (1 Cor. 15:53, 54; 1 Tim. 6:16).

Meaning of the attribute in Paul's writings

While the attribute of eternality denotes God's relationship to the ages of time, immortality is used in contrast to the reality of death which has entered this world (Rom. 5:12). The μόνος of 1 Timothy 6:16 declares God to be the only One who possesses immortality as an essential property.[24] He has an "absolute deathless existence."[25] It states negatively what ζωή and ζάω in relation to God state positively. It speaks of God as "life's never-failing fountain."[26] Therefore immortality speaks of an endless existence, but it also implies more than that. An immortal body is given to the believer so that he may enjoy the blissful state of immortality, which is connected with the idea of everlasting salvation and eternal blessedness.[27] The believer receives immortality as a gift but God possesses it. It belongs to God as an essential attribute and from His fountain of immortality the believer drinks.[28]

The Incorruptibility of God

The lexical basis

The revelation of this attribute centers around the use of ἀφθαρσία and the corresponding adjective ἄφθαρτος.

In classical Greek it referred to that which was incorruptible, undecaying, eternal, and immortal.[29] In early Greek philosophy it was used to denote that which abides and is immutable.[30] The related antonymn φθείρω meant to ruin, corrupt, and destroy. It could refer to not only physical corruption but also moral corruption.[31] Φθείρω and its cognates were used to speak of perishing in battle, dying of an illness, of buildings which crumble with age, of the disaster that a flood creates, of a ship that wrecks, of economic ruin, of milk that spoiled, and of fruit that is destroyed by insects.[32] In the moral realm it could refer to being seduced or bribed.[33] Ἄφθαρτος and ἀφθαρσία occur only in the apogrypha of the LXX (Wi. 2:23; 6:19; 4 Ma. 9:22, 17:12). The antonyms are primarily used for שחת. It could refer to both physical and moral corruption; and notable is the use of φθαρτός which refers to an animal sacrifice that is marred, defective, or blemished (Lev. 22:25). In the New Testament ἀφθαρσία is found seven times and always in Paul's writings (Rom. 2:7; 1 Cor. 15:42, 50, 53, 54; Eph. 6:24; 2 Tim. 1:10). Ἄφθαρτος is also used seven times in the New Testament. Four of these uses are in Paul (Rom. 1:23; 1 Cor. 9:25, 15:52; 1 Tim. 1:17) and the other three are in Peter's writings (1 Pet. 1:4, 23; 3:4).

Meaning of the attribute in Paul's writings

"It is a remarkable testimony to the reign of sin,

and therefore of imperfection, of decay, of death, throughout this whole fallen world, that as often as we desire to set forth the glory, purity, and perfection of that other higher world toward which we strive, we are almost inevitably compelled to do this by the aid of negatives, by the denying to that higher order of things the leading features and characteristics of this."[34] The quality of ἄφθαρτος that is ascribed to God (Rom. 1:23) includes the idea of immortality that ἀθανασία denotes, but it is more comprehensive than the latter term. It denotes not only that God is immortal but also that He is incorruptible in the moral as well as the physical realm. It negates the idea of any present corruption and also the possiblity of any future corruption. It views God in sharp contrast to man who is corruptible (Rom. 1:23). Man is corruptible not only in that his body is decaying (1 Cor. 15:42, 53, 54; 2 Cor. 4:6) but also in that he is liable to moral corruption (1 Cor. 15:33; 2 Cor. 11:13). It also views God in antithesis to Satan whose work is that of corrupting men's mind in contrast to God's work of renewing men's mind (Rom. 12:2). A yet further contrast is with the present creation which is in slavery to corruption (Rom. 8:21). Because God is incorruptible, His continuous work in the world (Eph. 1:11) and in His people (Phil. 2:13) puts no strain on Him as He is not subject to wear or decay. This quality is available to men through the gospel (2 Tim. 1:10) which extends the promise of an incorruptible body as well as soul (1 Cor. 15:50, 53, 54). The believer also is encouraged to live his life in such a way as to receive the price of incorruptible rewards (1 Cor. 9:25).

The Life of God

The lexical basis

The key terms are ζωή and ζάω. In classical Greek they denoted "the physical vitality of organic beings, animals, men and also plants."[35] As Bultmann puts it, "Life is understood, not as a thing, but as vitality, as the nature or manner which characterizes all living creatures as such."[36] "Life is associated with the self-movement of living creatures as opposed to mechanical movement."[37] In the LXX ζωή and ζάω were primarily used to translate חיים, חיה, and חי. A careful look at each of Paul's uses of these terms reveals his teaching concerning life as it relates to God.

Meaning of the attribute in Paul's writings

Ryrie states that "it is the living nature of God which assumed particular importance in Pauline thought."[38] To speak of God as the living God was to place him in contrast to the lifeless idols who are impotent to respond to the needs of their worshipers (1 Thess. 1:9; cf. Acts 14:15). It denotes that God is not idle but active in history carrying out His plan. As Bulcock states, "He is eternally living out what He is."[39] France writes:

> 'The living God' is not a synonym for 'He who is,' a metaphysical concept of God 'being there' (whether 'up there,' 'out there,' or anywhere else!). Life, in the Bible, means something vibrant and dynamic. It involves action. To speak of God as the living God is to make the daring claim that God is actively present here and now, a force to be reckoned with. If He is not that, then whether or not He exists is an academic question, with which the Bible is not concerned; at least He would not be <u>living</u>, and that is what matters. If He were not living, He could not be God, in any sense that would mean anything to the men of the Bible.[40]

It is an Old Testament concept and it is found in the Old Testament quotations in Romans 9:26 and 14:11. The Spirit who is actively at work in the believer's life is the Spirit of the living God (2 Cor. 3:3). Believers are termed the temple of the living God (2 Cor. 6:16) and the church of the living God (1 Tim. 3:15). It is the living God who is both the object of the believer's service (1 Thess. 1:9) as well as the believer's hope (1 Tim. 4:10).

The term "living God" also declared Him to be the author and sustainer of all life. Paul explicitly states that God gives life to all things in his letter to Timothy and in his preaching in Athens (1 Tim. 6:13; Acts 17:25). He even alludes to the Genesis account that records God's breathing life into Adam (1 Cor. 15:45; cf. Gen. 2:7). Thus He is the author of all life as well as the sustainer of all life (cf. Acts. 17:28; Col. 1:17). The emphasis, however, in Paul is on the eternal life that God possesses and gives to the believer. Eternal life denotes not only an endless duration of existence but also a special quality of life that characterized the personality of Jesus Christ.[41] In this sense ζωή sets forth "the blessedness of God and the blessedness of the creature in communion with God."[42] Men are declared to be alienated from the life of God (Eph. 4:18) and therefore dead (Eph. 2:1). However, it is Christ who abolished death and brought immortality and life to light through the gospel (2 Tim. 1:10). Life is both manifested in Christ and mediated through Him as the gospel is the "word of life" (Phil. 2:16), because it contains the promise of life in Christ Jesus (2 Tim. 1:1). Paul describes the believer's new life in Christ as a spiritual resurrection (Rom. 6:8; Eph. 2:5; Col. 2:13) and as an act of creation (2 Cor. 5:17; Eph. 2:10). It is enjoyed now as the believer walks in newness of life (Rom. 6:4), is alive to God (Rom. 6:11; cf. Eph. 4:18), and indwelt by Christ (Gal. 2:20; Col. 3:4). However, it is after the resurrection that the full state of immortality will be entered (1 Cor. 15:53; 2 Cor. 5:4). This eternal life is a gift of the living God (Rom. 6:23).

The Invisibility of God

The lexical basis

Ἀόρατος is a verbal adjective that in classical Greek referred to the unseen world or that which was invisible. It also later developed the sense of something one had not seen or that which one had no experience.[43] It is a rare word in the LXX. It appears only three times, and never is it directly attributed to God (Gen. 1:2; Isa. 45:3; 2 Macc. 9:5).[44] In the New Testament ἀόρατος occurs five times, and four of these are in Paul's writings (Rom. 1:20; Col. 1:15, 16; 1 Tim. 1:17). The other occurrence is in Hebrews 11:27. Of Paul's five uses all but Colossians 1:16 are a reference to God.

Meaning of the attribute in Paul's writings

"As an ascription of God, pagan literature has no parallel."[45] It is one of the attributes that is mentioned in the doxology of 1 Timothy 1:17. While Paul declares that no man has seen or can see God (1 Tim. 6:18), he does affirm that τα ἀόρατα αὐτοῦ can be clearly seen through God's creative work (Rom. 1:20). In other words while it is true that no one can see or has seen God's invisible essence, this essence has not remained entirely hidden as He has graciously revealed its contents. The invisible attributes which are signified by the τα ἀόρατα are further defined in Romans 1:20 as His eternal power and divine nature.[46] As an invisible spiritual being, God is distinguished from the material creation, but He has left the imprints of His glory upon His creative work. Some of His creation shares this invisible nature (Col. 1:16), but in spite of this similarity they are dissimilar in that they are regarded as created beings. The supreme revelation of the invisible God is in Christ, who is the image of the invisible God (Col. 1:15). It is not that the invisible essence has become visible for no man has seen God (1 Tim. 6:16), but it has been revealed. This revelation is referred to as an εἰκών, which denotes not a mere resemblance or ὁμοίωμα but a copy and reflection of the archetype.[47] It is the invisible God who is the author of the believer's hope, and a hope that is seen is not hope (Rom. 8:24; cf. Heb. 11:1). Likewise, it is the eternal nature of the invisible God that Paul fixed his spiritual eyes upon to comfort him in his suffering (2 Cor. 4:18).

The Omnipresence of God

The presence of the Lord in Paul's theology

This truth is not built upon a key word or words, but it is clearly developed. The presence of the Lord is seen in a variety of ways in Paul's writings. First, there is the universal presence of the Lord that Paul declared to his audience in Athens (Acts 17:27b-28a). This is also the interpretation that some give to the phrase in Ephesians 1:23 which declares that Christ "fills all in all." In interpreting this phrase Kent remarks, "He is the one who fills all the universe with all it contains and needs."[48] Likewise, according to Wood, Ephesians 4:10 denotes that Christ fills all things with "his presence and himself."[49] Romans 10:6-7 is cited by some[50] as teaching that God is omnipresent, but the main point in these verses is the accessibility of God's truth which Paul was preaching.[51] Secondly, there is the special presence of the Lord in and among His church. The fact of the indwelling Spirit is a test whether an individual belongs to the Lord (Rom. 8:9; cf. 1 Cor. 6:19; Gal. 2:20). Likewise, the corporate church is declared to be a dwelling place of God (Eph. 2:22) and a holy temple (Eph. 2:21). Thirdly, the presence of the Lord is spoken of in the sense of God being with His people to protect and help them.[52] It is seen in this sense in such passages as Romans 15:33, 2 Corinthians 13:11, Philippians 4:9, and 2 Thessalonians 3:16. Fourthly, there is His special presence in the incarnate Christ (Col. 2:9). Fifthly, there is His special presence in heaven (1 Tim. 6:16). It is this latter sense of God's presence that the believer is presently absent from (2 Cor. 5:6), but he looks forward to it with great anticipation because it will mean a more "intimate fellowship with Christ than he experiences on earth"[53] (2 Cor. 5:8; Phil. 1:23; 1 Thess. 4:17). This is what the unbeliever will be separated from for all eternity (2 Thess. 1:9).[54] The believer who will enjoy this blissful state in God's presence will clearly realize that he is a debtor to God's grace as there will be no boasting before Him (1 Cor. 1:29). It is in these five senses that the presence of the Lord is spoken of in Paul's writings. It can therefore be said that He is present with all but not with all in the same way.

The presence of the Lord in Paul's life

Paul constantly speaks of his life and ministry as being carried out "in the sight of God" (2 Cor. 2:17, 4:2,

7:12, 8:21, 12:19). He maintained that one of the marks of the true and sincere minister was that he consciously lives his life in the sight of God (2 Cor. 2:17, 4:2). Paul was not primarily concerned with defending himself before men, but his consciousness of God's presence freed him to be concerned for the upbuilding of those he ministered to and loved rather than his own reputation (2 Cor. 12:19). He also affirmed that the reference point of those he sought to correct was not himself but God (2 Cor. 7:12). The activities that Paul engaged in and encouraged others to participate in were those which were "good and acceptable in the sight of God" (1 Tim. 2:3, 5:4). When he solemnly charged Timothy to maintain the principle of his instruction without bias and to preach the word, he does so "under the very eye and with the full approval of God"[55] (1 Tim. 5:21, 6:13; 2 Tim. 4:1-2). This is the degree of seriousness with which Paul regarded his instructions to others, and he encouraged Timothy to follow his example in charging others "in the presence of God" (2 Tim. 2:14). While Paul did not disregard what was honorable and right in the sight of men (Rom. 12:17; 2 Cor. 8:21), he consciously lived his life under the direct gaze of the eyes of God. In light of this truth he urged all who name the name of the Lord to live a pure life and maintain their convictions before God (2 Tim. 2:19; Rom. 14:22).

Notes

[1]Hermann Cremer, Biblico-Theological Lexicon of New Testament Greek, p. 611.

[2]Ibid.

[3]Ernest De Witt Burton, A Critical and Exegetical Commentary on the Epistle to the Galatians, ICC, p. 426.

[4]TDNT, s.v. "αἰών," by Herman Sasse, 1 (1964):200.

[5]TNIDNTT, s.v. "αἰών," by J. Guhrt, 3 (1978):829.

[6]George Ricker Berry, Dictionary of New Testament Greek Synonyms, p. 35.

[7]Ibid.

[8]TNIDNTT, s.v. "αἰών," 3 (1978):830.

[9]TDNT, s.v. "αἰων," 1 (1964):199.

[10]Ibid. The expression αἰων αἰῶνος is probably related to the Hebrew עדי עד. Ibid., 1 (1964):200.

[11]Henry George Liddell and Robert Scott, A Greek-English Lexicon, s.v. "αἰώνιος," p. 45.

[12]James Hope Moulton and George Milligan, The Vocabulary of the Greek Testament, p. 16.

[13]William Barclay, New Testament Words, p. 35.

[14]TNIDNTT, s.v. "αἰών," 3 (1978):832.

[15]BAG, 4th rev. ed., s.v. "αἰώνιος," pp. 27-28.

[16]TDNT, s.v. "αἰώνιος," by Hermann Sasse, 1 (1964):209.

[17]TNIDNTT, s.v. "αἰών," 3 (1978):833.

[18]Sasse interprets it as "life-long" in this context. TDNT, s.v. "αἰώνιος," 1 (1964):209. However, the term may refer to the eternal relationship that now exists between Onesimus and Philemon.

[19]H. P. Liddon, Explanatory Analysis of St. Paul's First Epistle to Timothy, p. 7.

[20]Liddell and Scott, s.v. "ἀθανασία," p. 30.

[21]TDNT, s.v. ἀθανασία ," by Rudolph Bultmann, 3 (1965):22.

[22]Ibid., 3 (1965):24.

[23]Moulton and Milligan, p. 11.

[24]Liddon, p. 88.

[25]D. Edmond Hiebert, First Timothy, EBC, p. 119.

[26]Walter Hendriksen, Exposition of the Pastoral Epistles, NTC, p. 208.

[27]Ibid. [28]Ibid.

[29]Liddell and Scott, s.v. "ἀφθαρσία," p. 289.

[30]The immortal was found in the cosmos itself in early Greek philosophy but later it was attributed to that which is outside and above the world. TDNT, s.v. "φθείρω," by Günther Harder, 9 (1974):95-96.

[31]TNIDNTT, s.v. "φθείρω," by F. Merkel, 1 (1975):468.

[32]TDNT, s.v. "φθείρω," 9 (1974):94.

[33]Ibid.

[34]Richard C. Trench, Synonyms of the New Testament, p. 253.

[35]TDNT, s.v. "ζωή," by Rudolph Bultmann, 2 (1964): 832.

[36]Ibid. [37]Ibid., 2 (1964):833.

[38]Charles Caldwell Ryrie, Biblical Theology of the New Testament, p. 167.

[39]H. Bulcock, Religion and Its New Testament Expressions, p. 71.

[40]R. T. France, The Living God, p. 11.

[41]ZPBE, s.v. "Life," by W. B. Wallis, 3:927.

[42]Trench, p. 253.

[43]Liddell and Scott, s.v. "ἀορασία," p. 173.

[44]'Αορασία occurs in six passages and always carries the meaning of blindness.

[45]A. H. McNeile, New Testament Teaching in the Light of St. Paul's, p. 211.

[46]Θειότης in Romans 1:20 signifies God as a being who is possessed of divine attributes. It is distinguished from θεότης which denotes the divine personality. C. E. B. Cranfield, A Critical and Exegetical Commentary on the Epistle to the Romans, ICC, 2 vols., 1:115. Cf. Trench, pp. 7-10.

[47]T. K. Abbott, The Epistle to the Ephesians and the Colossians, ICC, p. 210.

[48]Homer Kent, Ephesians--The Glory of the Church, EBC, p. 32. Hodge also follows this interpretation. Charles Hodge, Systematic Theology, 3 vols.; vol. 1: Introduction--Theology Proper, p. 384.

[49]A. Skevington Wood, in EBC, 12 vols.; 11:58.

[50]ZPEB, s.v. "Omnipresence," by A. H. Leitch, 4:531.

[51]John Murray, The Epistle to the Romans, NIC, 2 vols., 2:55.

[52]C. E. B. Cranfield, A Critical and Exegetical Commentary on the Epistle to the Romans, ICC, 2 vols., 2:780.

[53]Murray J. Harris, in EBC, 12 vols.; 10:348.

[54]The ἀπό of 2 Thessalonians 1:9 is best taken in a local sense to denote separation as opposed to a causal sense which would simply indicate that the eternal punishment proceeds from God. D. Edmond Hiebert, The Thessalonian Epistles, p. 291. Thus, eternal punishment is viewed as being separated from "the Lord's favor and all which gives meaning and blessedness to life," Ibid., p. 292. It is of course also described with the use of such terms as wrath, indignation, and affliction.

[55]William Hendriksen, Exposition of Pastoral Epistles, NTC, p. 183.

CHAPTER VI

THE GLORY OF GOD IN PAULINE THEOLOGY

Lexical Basis

The term δόξα is found 165 times in the New Testament and 77 of these occurrences are in the Pauline Epistles.[1] In classical Greek it noted an opinion or judgment. It could note the opinion which one had of others or which others had of him and therefore could carry the sense of reputation or honor.[2] It is linked with δοκέω.[3] However, most agree that the concept of δόξα was transformed by the LXX and Aalen cites it as one of the clearest examples of the change in meaning of a Greek word when it came under the influence of the Bible.[4] It occurs some 280 times in the canonical books, and it is used for כבוד some 180 times.[5] It is for this reason that Kittel calls כבוד the "true and dominant equivalent of the LXX δόξα" and according to him δόξα "has become identical with כבוד."[6] The root meaning of כבוד is "heavy."[7] It can refer to wealth or riches (Gen. 31:1) and could be used to indicate a man of weight or substance (cf. Gen. 45: 13; Job 19:9). Thus a "heavy" man was a man of worth and honor. This worth and honor came to be associated not only with one's material substance but also with one's character and reputation. The Old Testament speaks of the glory or honor of one who fears God (Ps. 112:9), one who is wise (Prov. 3:16, 35; 8:18), humble (Prov. 15:33, 18:12, 22:4, 25:27, 29:23), one who keeps away from strife (Prov. 20:3), and one who is gracious (Prov. 11:16). The idea of splendor is also associated with כבוד and this sense can be seen in the magnificent garments of Aaron (Exod. 28:2) and the splendor of the temple (1 Chron. 22:5; Hag. 2:3, 7, 9). Out of this background כבוד became an appropriate term for God Himself. It signified His intrinsic worth and majestic splendor which demands honor. As Guthrie says, כבוד "came to have a special significance when applied to God."[8] He is the God of glory (Ps. 29:3) and the King of glory (Ps. 24:7, 8, 9, 10) because His name is glorious (Pss. 72:19, 145:5; Neh. 9:5). The emphasis is upon the manifestation of this glory in His creation (Ps. 19:1) and in His acts on behalf of His people (Exod. 16:7). The divine radiance that characterized His special presence in the cloud (Exod. 16:10), at the giving of the Law (Exod. 24:16), in the tabernacle (Exod. 40:34-35), and in the temple (Ezek. 10:4) are also a manifestation of His glory. The future age is full of references to כבוד in that it will be a display of God's glory or character in His works of judgment (Isa. 24:23; Ezek. 39:21), His glorious appearing (Isa. 60:1-2), and the declaration and knowledge of His glory to all the nations (Isa. 66:19; Hab. 2:14).

The primary meaning of δόξα emerges in its reference to God in the LXX.[9] It came to denote His "divine nature," and to glorify God meant "no other than an affirmation of this nature."[10] Its usage to denote this "divine and heavenly radiance," the "loftiness and majesty" of God, and the "being of God" arose out of its association with כבוד in the LXX.[11] Kittel states this point in this way:

> When the translator of the OT first thought of using δόξα for כבוד, he initiated a linguistic change of far-reaching significance, giving to the Greek term a distinctiveness of sense which could hardly be surpassed. Taking a word for opinion, which implies all the subjectivity and therefore all the vacillation of human views and conjectures, he made it express something absolutely objective, i.e., the reality of God.[12]

The Development of the Idea in Paul's Writing

The manifestation of God's invisible attributes is termed God's glory.[13] Ramm states that God's glory is "not an attribute of God but an attribute of God's total nature."[14] The heavenly splendor and majesty that proceeds from His attributes are also underscored by this term. Paul speaks of the glory or majesty[15] of the incorruptible God in Romans 1:23. He, likewise, speaks of the glory or splendor of His grace, which probably denotes, as Abbott insists, the glorious manifestation of His grace[16] (Eph. 1:6). Therefore, God is called the Father of glory not only because He is the One to whom all glory belongs but also because He is the source from which all the divine splendor and perfection proceed in their manifestation (Eph. 1:17).[17]

The emphasis in Paul is upon the manifestation of God in Christ. The Old Testament manifestation of the Shekinah glory is referred to in Romans 9:4 and 2 Corinthians 3:7. However, the manifestation of it in Christ is paramount. For this reason Paul refers to the glory of Christ who, as the very image of God, reflected His character (2 Cor. 4:4). In His coming, love and grace are said to have appeared (Titus 2:11, 3:4). Paul states that the rulers of this world crucified Christ and uses the title "Lord of glory" to magnify the crime (1 Cor. 2:8). However, it was the glory of the Father that raised Christ from the dead (Rom. 6:4), and it is in Christ that God makes known the riches of His glory to vessels of mercy (Rom. 9:23). While man was made in God's image and was meant to reflect His glory (1 Cor. 11:7), he has sinned and fallen short of God's glory, which in Romans 3:23 refers to his failure of reflecting the glory of God.[18] However, it is in Christ that the believer can be changed from glory to glory (2 Cor. 3:18), which is another Pauline way of stating conformity to the image of Christ (Rom. 8:29). This ultimate conformity, therefore, can be spoken of as the believer's glorification (Rom. 8:30), and many references to δόξα refer to this "state of blessedness into which believers are to enter hereafter through being brought into the likeness of Christ."[19] It is in this state that believers will reflect God's glory. This will follow Christ's glorious appearing (Titus 2:13) when He comes to be glorified in the saints as shown by the use of ἐνδοξάζω in 2 Thessalonians 1:10.

The response of man to the God who has revealed Himself is to glorify God. To glorify God does not mean to add something to God, but it is an active acknowledgment of who God is.[20] It means to "ascribe to God the glory that belongs to him as God, to give to him in thought, affection, and devotion the place that belongs to him."[21] It is the responsibility of all men as His glory has been shown to all through His work of creation; and the beginning of the devolution of man is that he did not glorify God (Rom. 1:21). It is the greater responsibility of the believer who has embraced the glorious gospel (1 Tim. 1:11) which enables him to gain the glory of Christ (2 Thess. 2:14). While in one sense even man's sin displays God's glory (Rom. 3:7) and all men will one day be forced to recognize who Christ is to the glory of God the Father (Phil. 2:11), believers are now to acknowledge God for who He is (cf. Rom. 4:20) that His name may be glorified in them (2 Thess. 1:12). It is the very resources of God's glory that empower the believer and provides for his needs (Eph. 3:16; Phil. 4:19; Col. 1:11); and the pattern set forth in Paul's writings is that the believer is to be alert to ascribe glory to God. Δόξα is used to denote Paul's praise to God for His sovereign plan (Rom. 11:36), Christ's acceptance of the believer (Rom. 15:7), His wisdom (Rom. 16:27), the truthfulness of His promises (2 Cor. 1:20), His transforming work of grace (2 Cor. 4:15), the death of Christ (Gal. 1:5), His ability to answer prayer

(Eph. 3:21), His mercy and grace (1 Tim. 1:17), and His deliverance from evil (2 Tim. 4:18).[22] Paul insists that all that God does is to the praise of His glory (Eph. 1:12, 14), and all the believer does is to be done to the glory of God (1 Cor. 10:31).

Notes

[1]TNIDNTT, s.v. "δόξα," by S. Aalen, 2 (1976):45.

[2]Henry George Liddell and Robert Scott, A Greek-English Lexicon, s.v. "δόξα," p. 444.

[3]Ibid.

[4]TNIDNTT, s.v. "δόξα," 2 (1976):44.

[5]TDNT, s.v. "δόξα," by Gerhard Kittel, 2 (1964):242.

[6]Ibid. [7]BDB, s.v. "כבד," p. 457.

[8]Donald Guthrie, New Testament Theology, p. 90.

[9]TDNT, s.v. "δόξα," 2 (1964):244.

[10]Ibid. [11]Ibid., 2 (1964):237.

[12]Ibid., 2 (1964):245.

[13]Norman L. Geisler, "God, Evil, and Dispensations," in Walvoord: A Tribute, ed. Donald Campbell, p. 97.

[14]Bernard Ramm, Them He Glorified, p. 18.

[15]BAG, 4th rev. ed., s.v. "δόξα," p. 202.

[16]T. K. Abbott, The Epistle to the Ephesians and to the Colossians, ICC, p. 10.

[17]W. E. Vine, An Expository Dictionary of New Testament Words, 4 vols., 2:153.

[18]John Murray, The Epistle to the Romans, NIC, 2 vols., 1:112-13. See also Guthrie, p. 91.

[19]Vine, 2:153. Such passages include Romans 2:7, 10; 5:2; 8:18, 21; 9:23; 1 Corinthians 2:7, 15:43; 2 Corinthians 4:17; Philippians 3:21; Colossians 1:27, 3:4; and 1 Thessalonians 2:12.

[20]TDNT, s.v. "δόξα," 2 (1964):248.

[21]Murray, 1:41.

[22]One might also observe the use of δοξάζω in Romans 15:6, 9; 1 Corinthians 16:20; 2 Corinthians 9:13; Galatians 1:24; and 2 Thessalonians 3:1. Related is the use of τιμή in 1 Timothy 1:17 and 6:16; the use of καυχάομαι in Romans 5:11, 1 Corinthians 1:31, and 2 Corinthians 10:17; and the use of εὐλογητός in Romans 1:25, 9:5; 2 Corinthians 1:3, 11:31; and Ephesians 1:3. For the more indirectly related idea of thanksgiving in Paul, see Peter T. Obrien, "Thanksgiving Within the Structure of Pauline Theology," in Pauline Studies, eds. Donald A. Hagner and Murray T. Harris, pp. 50-63. Obrien observes, "Paul mentions the subject of Thanksgiving more often per page than any other Hellenistic author, pagan or Christian" (61).

CHAPTER VII

CONCLUSION

It is almost impossible to overstate the importance of the doctrine of the character of God. "The only proper way to obtain perfectly reliable knowledge of the divine attributes is by the study of God's self-revelation in Scripture."[1] The task of this study has been to study this doctrine of the attributes of God in light of the revelation that comprises Pauline theology.[2] In light of both the importance of this doctrine in Pauline theology and the lack of attention that has been given it,[3] the contribution of this study has been a systematic exhibition of the incidental references that contribute to Paul's discussion of the attributes of God. This study examined God's knowledge, wisdom, love, mercy, grace, kindness, patience, truthfulness and faithfulness, righteousness, wrath, sovereignty, power, eternality, immortality, incorruptibility, life, invisibility, omnipresence, and glory. An attempt has been made to develop each attribute in a way that does justice to Paul's treatment of it. It is clear from Paul's writing that "the Being of God is characterized by a depth, a fullness, a variety, and a glory far beyond our comprehension."[4] As Ryrie has written, "Systematic Theology is as a blossom, each petal of which Biblical Theology has examined separately and in detail."[5] This study has been an attempt to examine the doctrine of God's attributes as it is contained in Pauline theology.

Paul does not discuss the attributes of God in a speculative way or as static qualities. In keeping with the living nature of God his emphasis is on the display of God's attributes. The unique thing about Paul's discussion of the attributes of God is that he writes of them from the perspective of the completed revelation of the incarnation and death of Christ. Christ is the very image of the invisible God (Col. 1:15). It is in Christ that God's knowledge and wisdom (Col. 2:3), love (Rom. 5:6-8), grace (Titus 2:11), righteousness (Rom. 3:25), power (Eph. 1:19-20), sovereign plan (Eph. 3:11), presence (Col. 2:9), truth (Eph. 4:21), and life (2 Tim. 1:1) are clearly seen. He also speaks of the display of God's attributes in relationship to his own life. As Sanday has said:

> St. Paul is himself the best commentary upon his own theology. His life was inspired by his theology and his theology is the reflection of his life. It is no scholastic system, worked out in the cold atmosphere of the study.[6]

In other words, he speaks of God's love (Gal. 2:20), mercy (1 Tim. 1:16), grace (1 Tim. 1:14), patience (1 Tim. 1:16), sovereignty (Gal. 1:15-16), power (Eph. 3:7), and presence (2 Cor. 4:2) from his personal experience. Indeed it is with a sense of awe that he discusses the attributes of God (Rom. 11:33). If one is looking for the secret of this man's life, it would have to be that "no man ever had an intenser or more vital sense of God."[7] He understood that all that God did displayed His glory (Eph. 1:12, 14) and that the task of man was to glorify God in all that he does (1 Cor. 10:31).

Notes

[1]Berkhof, Systematic Theology, p. 54.

[2]See pages 10-11 above.

[3]See pages 1-5 above.

[4]Berkhof, p. 42.

[5]Charles Caldwell Ryrie, Biblical Theology of the New Testament, p. 18.

[6]W. Sanday, "Some Leading Ideas in the Theology of St. Paul," The Expositor 8 (1878):58.

[7]A Dictionary of the Bible, s.v. "Predestination," by B. B. Warfield, 4:58.

BIBLIOGRAPHY

BIBLIOGRAPHY

Books

Abbott, T. K. A Critical and Exegetical Commentary on the Epistles to the Ephesians and to the Colossians. The International Critical Commentary. Edinburgh: T & T Clark, 1897.

Adeney, Walter F. The Theology of the New Testament. 2d ed. London: Hodder and Stoughton, 1895.

Alexander, S. A. The Christianity of St. Paul. London: Longmans, Green, and Company, 1899.

Amiot, Francois. The Key Concepts of St. Paul. 3d ed. Translated by John Pirgle. New York: Herder and Herder, 1963.

Barclay, William. Ambassador for Christ--the Life and Teaching of Paul. N.p.: Church of Scotland Youth Committee, 1951; reprint ed., Valley Forge: Judson Press, 1974.

________. The Letter to the Romans. 2d ed. The Daily Study Bible. Edinburgh: The Saint Andrew Press, 1957.

________. The Mind of St. Paul. London: Collins Press, 1958.

________. New Testament Words. Philadelphia: Westminster Press, 1974.

Barr, James. Biblical Words for Time. Naperville, Ill.: Alec R. Allenson, 1962.

Barrett, C. K. A Commentary on the Epistle to the Romans. Harper's New Testament Commentaries. New York, Evanston, and London: Harper and Row Publishers, 1957.

________. From First Adam to Last: A Study in Pauline Theology. London: Adam and Charles Black, 1962.

________. The First Epistle to the Corinthians. Harper New Testament Commentaries. New York and Evanston: Harper and Row Publishers, 1968.

________. The Second Epistle to the Corinthians. Harper New Testament Commentaries. New York, Evanston, San Francisco, and London: Harper and Row Publishers, 1973.

Beardslee, William A. Human Achievement and Divine Vocation in the Message of Paul. London: SCM Press, 1961.

Beker, J. Christian. Paul the Apostle: The Triumph of God in Life and Thought. Philadelphia: Fortress Press, 1980.

Berkhof, L. Systematic Theology. 4th ed. Grand Rapids: Wm. B. Eerdmans Publishing Company, 1941.

Bernard, Thomas Dehany. The Progress of Doctrine in the New Testament. N.p.: American Tract Society, 1896; reprint ed., Minneapolis: Klock & Klock Christian Publishers, 1978.

Beyschlag, Willibald. New Testament Theology or Historical Account of the Teaching of Jesus and of Primitive Christianity According to New Testament Sources. 2 vols. Translated by Neil Buchanan. Edinburgh: T & T Clark, 1899.

Bonsirven, Joseph. Theologie du Nouveau Testament. Paris: Aubler, 1951.

Bornkamm, Gunther. Early Christian Experience. Articles translated by Paul L. Hammer from Das Ende des Gesetzes. 5th ed. Munich: Christian Kaiser Kerlag, 1966; and Studien zu Antike Und Urchristentum, 2d ed. Munich: Christian Kaiser Kerlag. New York and Evanston: Harper and Row Publishers, 1969.

Brox, Norbert. Understanding the Message of Paul. Translated by Joseph Blenkinsopp. Notre Dame: University of Notre Dame Press, 1968.

Bruce, Alexander Balmain. St. Paul's Conception of Christianity. Edinburgh: T & T Clark, 1894.

Bruce, F. F. The New Testament Development of Old Testament Themes. Grand Rapids: Wm. B. Eerdmans Publishing Company, 1968.

________. Paul and Jesus. Grand Rapids: Baker Book House, 1974.

________. Paul: Apostle of the Heart Set Free. Grand Rapids: Wm. B. Eerdmans Publishing Company, 1977.

Brunot, Amédée. Saint Paul and His Message. Translated by Ronald Matthews. New York: Hawthorn Books, 1959.

Bulcock, H. Religion and Its New Testament Expressions. London: Williams and Norgate, 1928.

Bultmann, Rudolf. Theology of the New Testament. 2 vols. Translated by Kendrick Grobel. London: SCM Press, 1952.

Burton, Ernest De Witt. A Critical and Exegetical Commentary on the Epistle to the Galatians. The International Critical Commentary. Edinburgh: T & T Clark, 1921.

Cerfaux, Lucien. The Spiritual Journey of Saint Paul. Translated by John C. Guinness. New York: Shedd and Word, 1968.

Chafer, Lewis Sperry. Systematic Theology. 8 vols. Dallas: Dallas Seminary Press, 1947-48.

Charnock, Stephen. Discourses Upon the Existence and Attributes of God. 2 vols. N.p.: Robert Carter and Brothers, 1853; reprint ed., Grand Rapids: Baker Book House, 1979.

Clarke, James Freeman. The Ideas of the Apostle Paul. Boston and New York: Haughton, Mifflin and Company, 1895.

Cohu, J. R. S. Paul in the Light of Modern Research. New York: Longmans, Green and Company, 1911.

Conzelmann, Hans. Grundiss der Theologie des Neuev Testaments. Munchen: Chr. Kaiser, 1967.

Cranfield, C. E. B. A Critical and Exegetical Commentary on the Epistle to the Romans. 2 vols. The International Critical Commentary. Edinburgh: T & T Clark, 1975-79.

Dahl, Nils Alstrup. Studies in Paul--Theology for the Early Christian Mission. Minneapolis: Augsburg Publishing House, 1977.

Davies, W. D. Paul and Rabbinic Judaism: Some Rabbinic Elements in Pauline Theology. Philadelphia: Fortress Press, 1980.

Deismann, Adolf. Paul. A Study in Social and Religious History. 2d ed. Translated by William E. Wilson. New York: George H. Doran Company, 1925.

Dodd, C. H. The Meaning of Paul for Today. New York: Meridian Books, 1957.

________. New Testament Studies. Manchester: Manchester University Press, 1953.

Dunn, James D. G. Unity and Diversity in the New Testament. Philadelphia: The Westminster Press, 1977.

Eadie, John. Commentary on the Epistle of Paul to the Colossians. N.p.: Richard Griffin and Company, 1856; reprint ed., Minneapolis: James and Klock Publishing Company, 1977.

________. Commentary on the Epistle to the Ephesians. Edinburgh: T. and T. Clark, 1883; reprint ed., Minneapolis: James and Klock Christian Publishers, 1977.

Ellis, E. Earle. Prophecy and Hermeneutic in Early Christianity. Grand Rapids: Wm. B. Eerdmans Publishing Company. 1978.

Farrar, F. W. The Life and Work of St. Paul. New York: E. P. Dutton and Company, 1883.

Feine, Paul. St. Paul as a Theologian. 2 vols. New York: Eaton and Mains, 1908.

Fitzmyer, Joseph A. Pauline Theology: A Brief Sketch. Englewood Cliffs, N.J.: Prentice-Hall, 1967.

France, R. T. The Living God. London: Inter-Varsity Press, 1970.

Furnish, Victor Paul. Theology and Ethics in Paul. New York: Abingdon Press, 1968.

Garrie, Alfred E. Studies of Paul and His Gospel. London: Hodder and Stoughton, 1911.

George, A. R. Communion with God. London: The Epworth Press, 1953.

Gibbs, John G. Creation and Redemption: A Study in Pauline Theology. Leiden: E. J. Brill, 1971.

Giblin, Charles Homer. In Hope of God's Glory: Pauline Theological Perspectives. New York: Herder and Herder, 1970.

Godet, F. Commentary on First Corinthians. Edinburgh: T. & T. Clark, 1889; reprint ed., Grand Rapids: Kregel Publications, 1977.

________. Commentary on the Epistle to the Romans. N.p.: Funk and Wagnall, 1883; reprint ed., Grand Rapids: Zondervan Publishing House, 1969.

Goodwin, Frank J. A Harmony of the Life of St. Paul. Grand Rapids: Baker Book House, 1951.

Gould, Ezra P. The Biblical Theology of the New Testament. London: The Macmillan Company, 1901.

Grant, Frederick C. An Introduction to New Testament Thought. New York and Nashville: Abingdon-Cokesbury Press, 1950.

Guthrie, Donald. New Testament Introduction. 3d ed., revised in one volume. Downers Grove, Ill.: Inter-Varsity Press, 1970.

________. New Testament Theology. Downers Grove, Ill.: Inter-Varsity Press, 1981.

Hagner, Donald A., and Harris, Murray J., eds. Pauline Studies. 1st American ed. Grand Rapids: Wm. B. Eerdmans Publishing Company, through special arrangement with the Paternostra Press, 1980.

Hanson, Anthony Tyrell. Studies in Paul's Teachings and Theology. London: S.P.C.K., 1974.

Harris, Murray J. "Second Corinthians." In The Expositor's Bible Commentary, 10 (1976):299-406. Edited by Frank E. Gaebelein. 12 vols. Grand Rapids: Zondervan Publishing House, 1976- .

Headlam, Arthur C. St. Paul and Christianity. New York: Longmans, Green, and Company, 1913.

Hendriksen, William. Exposition of Ephesians. New Testament Commentary. Grand Rapids: Baker Book House, 1967.

________. Exposition of Galatians. New Testament Commentary. Grand Rapids: Baker Book House, 1968.

________. Exposition of Philippians. New Testament Commentary. Grand Rapids: Baker Book House, 1967.

________. Exposition of the Pastoral Epistles. New Testament Commentary. Grand Rapids: Baker Book House, 1957.

________. Exposition of I and II Thessalonians. New Testament Commentary. Grand Rapids: Baker Book House, 1955.

Hiebert, D. Edmond. First Timothy. Everyman's Bible Commentary. Chicago: Moody Press, 1957.

________. Second Timothy. Everyman's Bible Commentary. Chicago: Moody Press, 1958.

________. The Thessalonian Epistles. Chicago: Moody Press, 1971.

________. Titus and Philemon. Everyman's Bible Commentary. Chicago: Moody Press, 1957.

Hodge, Charles. An Exposition of the First Epistle to the Corinthians. N.p.: n.d.; reprint ed., Grand Rapids: Wm. B. Eerdmans Publishing Company, 1974.

________. Commentary on the Epistle to the Romans. N.p.; 1886; reprint ed., Grand Rapids: Wm. B. Eerdmans Publishing Company, 1950.

________. Systematic Theology. 3 vols. N.p.: n.d.; reprint ed., Grand Rapids: Wm. B. Eerdmans Publishing Company, 1979.

Holtzmann, Heinrich Julius. Lehrbuch der Neutestamentlichen Theologie. 2 vols. Leipzig: J. C. B. Mohr, 1897.

Hunter, A. M. Interpreting Paul's Gospel. London: SCM Press, 1954.

________.Introducing New Testament Theology. London: SCM Press, 1957.

Käsemann, Ernst. New Testament Questions of Today. Philadelphia: Fortress Press, 1969.

Keck, Leander E. Paul and His Letters. Proclamation Commentaries. Philadelphia: Fortress Press, 1979.

Kennedy, H. A. A. The Theology of the Epistles. London: Duckworth and Company, 1919.

Kent, Homer A. The Pastoral Epistles: Studies in I and II Timothy and Titus. Chicago: Moody Press, 1958.

Klausner, Joseph. From Jesus to Paul. Translated by William F. Stinespring. New York: The Macmillan Company, 1943.

Knox, Wilfred L. St. Paul and the Church of the Gentiles. Cambridge: Cambridge University Press, 1939.

Kümmel, Werner Georg. The Theology of the New Testament According to Its Major Witnesses: Jesus--Paul--John. Translated by John E. Steely. Nashville and New York: Abingdon Press, 1973.

Ladd, George Eldon. A Theology of the New Testament. Grand Rapids: Wm. B. Eerdmans Publishing Company, 1974.

Lehman, Chester K. Biblical Theology. 2 vols. Scottdale, Pa.: Herald Press, 1971-74.

Lenski, R. C. H. The Interpretation of St. Paul's First and Second Epistles to the Corinthians. Minneapolis: Augsburg Publishing House, 1963.

________. The Interpretation of St. Paul's Epistles to the Galatians, to the Ephesians, and to the Philippians. Minneapolis: Augsburg Publishing House, 1961.

________. The Interpretation of St. Paul's Epistle to the Romans. Minneapolis: Augsburg Publishing House, 1961.

Liddon, H. P. Explanatory Analysis of St. Paul's Epistle to the Romans. London: Longmans, Green and Company, 1899; reprint ed., Minneapolis: James and Klock Christian Publishing Company, 1977.

________. Explanatory Analysis of St. Paul's First Epistle to Timothy. N.p.: Longmans, Green, and Company, 1897; reprint ed., Minneapolis: Klock & Klock Christian Publishers, 1978.

Lightfoot, J. B. Saint Paul's Epistles to the Colossians and to Philemon. N.p.: Macmillan and Company, 1879; reprint ed., Grand Rapids: Zondervan Publishing House, 1959.

________. St. Paul's Epistle to the Philippians. London: Macmillan and Company, 1913; reprint ed., Grand Rapids:

Lightner, Robert P. The First Fundamental: God. Nashville: Thomas Nelson, 1973.

Longenecker, Richard N. The Ministry and Message of Paul. Grand Rapids: Zondervan Publishing House, 1971.

________. Paul, Apostle of Liberty. N.p.: Harper and Row, Publishers, 1964; reprint ed., Grand Rapids: Baker Book House, 1976.

Longenecker, Richard N., and Tenney, Merrill C., eds. New Dimensions in New Testament Study. Grand Rapids: Zondervan Publishing House, 1974.

Manson, T. W. On Paul and John. Naperville, Ill.: Alec R. Allenson, 1963.

McDonald, H. D. Living Doctrines of the New Testament. N.p.: Pickering and Inglis, n.d.; reprint ed., Grand Rapids: Zondervan Publishing House, 1972.

McNeile, A. H. New Testament Teaching in the Light of St. Paul's. Cambridge: Cambridge University Press, 1923.

________. St. Paul: His Life, Letters, and Christian Doctrine. Cambridge: Cambridge University Press, 1925.

Mare, W. Harold. "First Corinthians." In The Expositor's Bible Commentary, 10 (1976):173-297. Edited by Frank E. Gaebelein. 12 vols. Grand Rapids: Zondervan Publishing House, 1976- .

Moffatt, James. Grace in the New Testament. New York: Ray Long and Richard R. Smith, Inc., 1932.

________. Love in the New Testament. London: Hodder and Stoughton, 1929.

Morgan, W. The Religion and Theology of the New Testament. Edinburgh: T. & T. Clark, 1917.

Morris, Leon. The Apostolic Preaching of the Cross. Grand Rapids: Wm. B. Eerdmans Publishing Company, 1955.

Moule, H. C. G. Studies in Colossians and Philemon. Kregel Popular Commentary Series. Cambridge: Cambridge University Press, 1893; reprint ed., Grand Rapids: Kregel Publications, 1977.

________. Studies in Ephesians. Kregel Popular Commentary Series. Cambridge: Cambridge University Press, 1893; reprint ed., Grand Rapids: Kregel Publications, 1977.

________. Studies in Philippians. Kregel Popular Commentary Series. Cambridge: Cambridge University Press, 1893; reprint ed., Grand Rapids: Kregel Publications, 1977.

________. Studies in Romans. Kregel Popular Commentary Series. Cambridge: Cambridge University Press, 1892; reprint ed., Grand Rapids: Kregel Publications, 1977.

________. Studies in II Timothy. Kregel Popular Commentary Series. London: Religious Tract Society, n.d.; reprint ed., Grand Rapids: Kregel Publications, 1977.

Moxnes, Halver. Theology in Conflict: Studies in Paul's Understanding of God in Romans. Leiden: E. S. Brill, 1980.

Müller, Jac. J. The Epistles of Paul to the Philippians and to Philemon. The New International Commentary on the New Testament. Grand Rapids: Wm. B. Eerdmans Publishing Company, 1955.

Murray, John. The Epistle to the Romans. 2 vols. The New International Commentary. Grand Rapids: Wm. B. Eerdmans Publishing Company, 1965-69.

Pfleiderer, Otto. Paulinism: A Contribution to the History of Primitive Christian Theology. 2 vols. Translated by Edward Peters. London and Edinburgh: Williams and Norgate, 1877.

Pierce, C. A. Conscience in the New Testament: A Study of Syneidesis in the New Testament, in the Light of Its Sources, and with Particular Reference to St. Paul with Some Observations Regarding Its Pastoral Relevance Today. London: SCM Press, 1955.

Prat, Fernand. The Theology of St. Paul. 2 vols. Translated by John L. Stoddard. London: Burns, Oates, and Washburn, 1957.

Radmacher, Earl D. You and Your Thoughts--The Power of Right Thinking. Wheaton: Tyndale House Publishers, 1977.

Rall, Harris F. According to Paul. New York: Charles Scribner's Sons, 1944.

Ramsay, W. M. The Teaching of Paul in Terms of the Present Day. London, New York, and Toronto: Hodder and Stoughton, 1973.

Richards, J. McDowell, ed. Soli Deo Gloria--New Testament Studies in Honor of William Childs Robinson. Richmond, Va.: John Knox Press, 1968.

Richardson, Alan. An Introduction to the Theology of the New Testament. London: SCM Press, 1958.

Ridderbos, Herman N. The Epistle of Paul to the Churches of Galatia. The New International Commentary. Grand Rapids: Wm. B. Eerdmans Publishing Company, 1953.

________. Paul and Jesus--Origin and General Character of Paul's Preaching of Christ. Translated by David H. Freeman. Nutley, N.J.: Presbyterian and Reformed Publishing Company, 1957.

________. Paul--An Outline of His Theology. Translated by John Richard De Witt. Grand Rapids: Wm. B. Eerdmans Publishing Company, 1975.

Robertson, A. T. Paul The Interpreter of Christ. New York: George H. Doran Company, 1921.

Robertson, Archibald, and Plummer, Alfred. A Critical and Exegetical Commentary on the First Epistle of St. Paul to the Corinthians. 2d ed. International Critical Commentary. Edinburgh: T & T Clark, 1914.

Rolston, Holmes, Consider Paul: Apostle of Jesus Christ. Richmond: John Knox Press, 1951.

Ross, D. M. The Faith of St. Paul: A Study of St. Paul as the Interpretor of Jesus. London: James Clarke and Company, n.d.

Ryrie, Charles Caldwell. Biblical Theology of the New Testament. Chicago: Moody Press, 1959.

________. Dispensationalism Today. Chicago: Moody Press, 1965.

Sabatier, A. The Apostle Paul: A Sketch of the Development of His Doctrine. 6th ed. Translated by A. M. Hellier. London: Hodder and Stoughton, 1906.

Salmond, S. D. F. "The Epistle of Paul to the Ephesians." In The Expositor's Greek Testament, 3:201-395. Edited by W. Robertson Nicoll. 5 vols. London: Hodder and Stoughton, 1900-10; reprint ed., Grand Rapids: Wm. B. Eerdmans Publishing Company, 1974.

Sanday, William, and Headlam, Arthur C. A Critical and Exegetical Commentary on the Epistle to the Romans. 5th ed. International Critical Commentary. Edinburgh: T & T Clark, 1902.

Schelkle, Karl Hermann. Theology of the New Testament. 4 vols. Translated by W. A. Jurgens. Collegeville, Minn.: Liturgical Press, 1971.

Schmid, Christian Friedrich. Biblical Theology of the New Testament. 3d. ed. Translated by G. H. Venables. Edinburgh: T & T Clark, 1882.

Schnackenburg, Rudolf, La Theologie du Nouveau Testament. Paris: Desclee De Brouwer, 1961.

Scott, Charles A. Anderson. Christianity According to Saint Paul. Cambridge: Cambridge University Press, 1961.

Shedd, William G. T. A Critical and Doctrinal Commentary on the Epistle of St. Paul to the Romans. N.p.: Charles Scribner's Sons, 1879; reprint ed., Minneapolis: Klock and Klock Christian Publishers, 1978.

________. Dogmatic Theology. 4 vols. N.p.: Charles Scribner's Sons, 1889; reprint ed., Minneapolis: Klock and Klock Christian Publishers, 1979.

Sheldon, Henry C. New Testament Theology. New York: Macmillan Company, 1911.

Simpson, E. K., and Bruce, F. F. Commentary on the Epistles to the Ephesians and Colossians. The New International Commentary of the New Testament. Grand Rapids: Wm. B. Eerdmans Publishing Company, 1957.

Stacey, W. D. The Pauline View of Man. London: MacMillan, 1956.

Stagg, Frank. New Testament Theology. Nashville: Broadman Press, 1962.

Stauffer, Ethelbert. New Testament Theology. Translated by John Marsh. London: SCM Press, 1955.

Stevens, George Barker. The Pauline Theology--A Study of the Origins and Correlation of the Doctrinal Teachings of the Apostle Paul. Rev. ed. New York: Charles Scribner's Sons, 1906.

________. The Theology of the New Testament. 2d ed. Edinburgh: T & T Clark, 1918.

Stewart, James S. A Man in Christ the Vital Elements of St. Paul's Religion. N.p.: Harper and Row, Publishers, n.d.; reprint ed., Grand Rapids: Baker Book House, 1975.

Stifler, James M. The Epistle to the Romans. Chicago: Moody Press, 1960.

Stott, John R. W. God's New Society. The Bible Speaks Today. Downers Grove, Ill.: Inter-Varsity Press, 1979.

Strong, Augustus H. Systematic Theology. Valley Forge: Judson Press, 1907.

Swete, Harry Barclay, ed. Essay on Some Biblical Questions of the Day. London: MacMillan and Company, 1909.

Taylor, Michael J., ed. A Companion to Paul: Readings in Pauline Theology. New York: Alba House, 1975.

Thiessen, Henry Clarence. Introductory Lectures in Systematic Theology. Grand Rapids: Wm. B. Eerdmans Publishing Company, 1977.

Thomas, W. H. Griffith. Studies in Colossians and Philemon. Grand Rapids: Baker Book House, 1973.

Towns, Elmer L., ed. A History of Religious Educators. Grand Rapids: Baker Book House, 1975.

Tozer, A. W. The Knowledge of the Holy. New York, Evanston, and London: Harper and Row Publishers, 1961.

Trench, Richard Chenevix. Synonyms of the New Testament. 9th ed. London: n.p., 1880; reprint ed., Grand Rapids: Wm. B. Eerdmans Publishing Company, 1953.

Vos, Geerhardus. The Pauline Eschatology. N.p.: Princeton University Press, 1930; reprint ed., Grand Rapids: Baker Book House, 1979.

Ward, J. W. C. What St. Paul Really Said. New York: Shocken Books, 1969.

Weidner, Revere Franklin. Biblical Theology of the New Testament. 2 vols. 2d rev. ed. Chicago, New York, Toronto, London, and Edinburgh: Fleming H. Revell Company, 1891.

Weiss, Bernhard. Biblical Theology of the New Testament. 2 vols. 3d ed. Translated by James E. Duguid. Edinburgh: T & T Clark, 1893.

Weinel, H. Biblische Theologie des Neuen Testaments: Die Religion Jesu und des Urchristentums. 4th ed. Tubingen: J. C. B. Mohr, 1928.

Westcott, Brooke Foss. Saint Paul's Epistle to the Ephesians. N.p.: Macmillan and Company, 1906; reprint ed., Minneapolis: Klock and Klock Christian Publishers, 1978.

Whately, Richard. Essays on Some of the Difficulties in the Writings of the Apostle Paul and in Other Parts of the New Testament. 8th ed. Andover: Warren F. Draper, 1865.

Whiteley, D. E. H. The Theology of St. Paul. Oxford: Basil Blackwell, 1966.

Wilder, Amos N. New Testament Faith for Today. London: SCM Press, 1954.

Wobbe, J. Der Charis-Gedanke Bei Paulus. Munster: Verlag der Aschendorffschen Verlagsbuchandlung, 1932.

Wood, A. Skevington. "Ephesians." In The Expositor's Bible Commentary, 11 (1978):3-92. Edited by Frank E. Gaebelein. 12 vols. Grand Rapids: Zondervan Publishing House, 1976- .

Young, Edward J. The Book of Isaiah. 3 vols. The New International Commentary of the Old Testament. Grand Rapids: Wm. B. Eerdmans Publishing Company, 1972.

Zeisler, J. A. The Meaning of Righteousness in Paul: A Linguistic and Theological Enquiry. Cambridge: Cambridge University Press, 1972.

Dictionaries, Encyclopedias, and Periodicals

Allan, John A. "The Will of God in Paul." Expository Times 72 (1960-61):142-45.

Baker's Dictionary of Theology. Edited by Everett F. Harrison, 1960 ed. S.v. "Authority," by W. C. G. Proctor, pp. 80-81; s.v. "Call, called, calling," by James J. Packer, pp. 108-9; s.v. "Decrees, eternal," by George N. M. Collins, p. 160; s.v. "Elect, election," by John Murray, pp. 180-81; s.v. "Faithful, faithfulness," by David A. Hubbard, pp. 211-12; s.v. "Foreknowledge," by Loraine Boettner, p. 225; s.v. "God," by Gorden H. Clark, pp. 238-48; s.v. "Grace," by T. H. L. Parker, pp. 257-58; s.v. "Immortality," by David W. Kerr, pp. 280-81; s.v. "Kind, kindness," by J. Theodore Mueller, p. 309; s.v. "Knowledge," by Gordon H. Clark, pp. 314-16; s.v. "Life," by J. Clement Connell, pp. 232-24; s.v. "Longsuffering," by Burton L. Goddard, p. 328; s.v. "Love," by Edward John Cornell, pp. 332-33; s.v. "Mercy," by Burton L. Goddard, p. 348; s.v. "Might," by L. E. H. Stephens-Hodge, p. 351; s.v. "Patience," by Richard E. Higginson, p. 396; s.v. "Power, powers," by Donald Guthrie, pp. 411-12; s.v. "Predestination," by Loraine Boettner, pp. 415-17; s.v. "Presence, Divine," by Geoffrey W. Bromiley, pp. 418-19; s.v. "Providence," by T. H. L. Parker, pp. 426-27; s.v. "Purpose," by Kenneth S. Kantzer, p. 431; s.v. "Right, righteousness," by

David Broughton Knox, pp. 461-62; s.v. "Truth," by Gordon H. Clark, pp. 532-33; s.v. "Will of God," by W. Stanford Reid, pp. 552-53; s.v. "Wrath," by William Childs Robinson, pp. 561-62.

Barre, Michael L. "'Fear of God' and the World View of Wisdom." Biblical Theology Bulletin 11 (April 1981): 41-43.

Bedenbaugh, J. Benjamin. "Paul's Use of 'Wrath of God.'" Lutheran Quarterly 6 (February 1954):154-57.

Biblico-Theological Lexicon of New Testament Greek. By Hermann Cremer. Translated by William Urwick, 4th English ed.

Blakely, E. H. "The Righteousness of God." The Expository Times 6 (1894-1895):45-46.

Bollier, John A. "The Righteousness of God." Interpretation 8 (October 1954):404-13.

Bosworth, Edward I. "The Influence of the Damascus Vision Upon Paul's Theology." Bibliotheca Sacra 56 (April 1899):278-300.

Boys-Smith, E. P. "St. Paul's Equivalent for the Kingdom of God." The Expository Times 12 (1900-1901):380-82.

Bring, Ragnar. "Paul and the Old Testament." Studia Theologica 25 (1971):21-60.

Brockington, L. H. "The Presence of God." The Expository Times 57 (1945-46):21-25.

Bruce, F. F. "Paul on Immortality." Scottish Journal of Theology 24 (1971):457-72.

Carr, Arthur. "St. Paul's Attitude Towards Greek Philosophy." The Expositor 5:9 (1899):372-81.

________. "Truth in Jesus: The Revelation of Christ and the Example of Christ." The Expositor 6:3 (1901):118-27.

Clark, Kenneth W. "The Meaning of Ἐνεργέω and Καταργέω in the New Testament." Journal of Biblical Literature 54 (1935):93-102.

Cobb, W. H. "Αἰώνιος, II Cor. iv. 17 and v. 1." Journal of Biblical Literature (June and December 1883):61.

A Concordance to the Greek Testament. Edited by W. F. Moulton and A. S. Geden, 4th ed.

A Concordance to the Septuagint and the Other Greek Versions of the Old Testament (Including the Apocryphal Books). 2 vols. By Edwin Hatch and Henry A. Redpath.

Dahl, Nils Alstrop. "The Neglected Factor in New Testament Theology." Reflection 73 (November 1975):5-8.

A Dictionary of New Testament Greek Synonyms. By George Ricker Berry.

Dods, Marcus. "St. Paul's View of the Greek Gods." The Expositor 5:1 (1895):237-40.

Dorfried, Karl Paul. "Justification and Last Judgment in Paul." Interpretation 30 (April 1976):140-52.

Drummond, James. "On the Meaning of 'Righteousness of God' in the Theology of St. Paul." The Hiebert Journal 1 (1902):83-95, 272-93.

Everts, William Walling. "Paul's Treatment of Knowledge." The Review and Expositor 18 (October 1921):416-27.

An Expository Dictionary of New Testament Words with Their Precise Meanings for English Readers. 4 vols. By W. E. Vine.

Forster, A. Haire. "The Meaning of Power for St. Paul." Anglican Theological Review 32 (1950):177-85.

Giblin, Charles H. "Three More Theistic Texts in Paul." Catholic Biblical Quarterly 37 (October 1975):527-47.

A Greek-English Lexicon. By Henry George Liddell and Robert Scott, new 9th ed.

A Greek-English Lexicon of the New Testament and Other Early Christian Literature. By Walter Bauer. Translated by William F. Arndt and Wilbur Gingrich, 4th rev. ed.

Hanson, R. P. C. "The Wrath of God." The Expository Times 58 (1946-47):216-18.

Hebert, Gabriel. "'Faithfulness' and 'Faith.'" Theology 58 (October 1955):373-79.

A Hebrew and English Lexicon of the Old Testament. By Francis Brown, S. R. Driver, and Charles A. Briggs.

Jamison, Leland. "Δικαιοσύνη in the Usage of Paul." The Journal of Bible and Religion 21 (January 1953):93-99.

Jeremias, J. "The Key to Pauline Theology." The Expository Times 76 (October 1964):27-30.

Johnson, S. Lewis, Jr. "God Gave Them Up. A Study in Divine Retribution." Bibliotheca Sacra 129 (April-June 1972): 124-33.

________. "Paul and the Knowledge of God." Bibliotheca Sacra 129 (January-March 1972):61-74.

________. "Studies in Romans--Part VIII. Divine Faithfulness, Divine Judgment, and the Problem of Antinomianism." Bibliotheca Sacra 130 (October-December 1973):329-37.

Kennedy, H. A. A. "St. Paul's Conception of the Knowledge of God." The Expositor 8:16 (1918):241-69.

Lofthouse, W. F. "The Righteousness of God." The Expository Times 50 (1938-39):441-45.

McCasland, S. Vernon. "'The Image of God' According to Paul." Journal of Biblical Literature 69 (March-December 1950):85-100.

A Manual Greek Lexicon of the New Testament. By G. Abbott-Smith.

Martin, Alfred J. "The Sovereignty of Grace as Seen in Romans 8:28-30." Bibliotheca Sacra 99 (October-December 1942): 453-68.

Mason, Clarence E. "A Study of Pauline Motives." Bibliotheca Sacra 111 (July 1954):213-28.

McKenzie, John L. "Natural Law in the New Testament." Biblical Research 9 (1964):3-13.

Morris, Leon. "Paul, Apostle of Love." Christianity Today 21 (September 1977):76, 78.

________. "The Wrath of God." The Expository Times 63 (1951-52):142-45.

The New Bible Dictionary. Edited by J. D. Douglas. 1962 ed. S.v. "Authority," by J. I. Packer, pp. 111-13; s.v. "Call, calling," by M. R. W. Farrer, pp. 180-81; s.v. "Election," by J. I. Packer, pp. 357-61; s.v. "God," by R. A. Finlayson, pp. 474-77; s.v. "Grace, favor," by J. H. Stringer, pp. 491-93; s.v. "Knowledge," by M. H. Cressey, pp. 702-3; s.v. "Life," by E. E. Ellis, pp. 735-39; s.v. "Longsuffering," by F. S. Fitzsimmonds, p. 745; s.v. "Love, beloved," by

F. H. Palmer, pp. 752-54; s.v. "Mercy, merciful," by J. W. C. Hoad, p. 709; s.v. "Patience," by J. W. C. Hoad, pp. 938-39; s.v. "Power," by R. E. Nixon, p. 1017; s.v. "Predestination," by J. I. Packer, pp. 1024-26; s.v. "Providence," by J. I. Packer, pp. 1050-52; s.v. "Righteousness," by D. B. Knox, p. 1097; s.v. "Time," by M. H. Cressey, pp. 1277-79; s.v. "Truth," by F. H. Palmer, pp. 1301-2; s.v. "Wisdom," by D. A. Hubbard, pp. 1333-34; s.v. "Wrath," by R. V. G. Tasker, p. 1341.

The New International Dictionary of New Testament Theology. Edited by Colin Brown, 1975-78. S.v. "ἀγαπάω," by W. Günther and H. C. Link, 2 (1976):538-51; s.v. "αἰών," by T. Guhrt, 3 (1978):826-33; s.v. "ἀλήθεια," by A. C. Thiselton, 3 (1978):874-902; s.v. "ἀνέχομαι," by V. Falkenroth and C. Brown, 2 (1976): 765-67; s.v. "βούλομαι," by D. Mueller, 3 (1978):1018-23; s.v. "γινώσκω," by E. D. Schmitz, 2 (1976):392-406; s.v. "δικαιοσύνη," by H. Seebass and Colin Brown, 3 (1978): 352-73; s.v. "δόξα," by S. Aulen, 2 (1976):44-52; s.v. "δύναμις," by O. Betz 2 (1976):601-6; s.v. "ἐκλέγομαι," by L. Coenen, 1 (1975):271-76; s.v. "ἔλεος," by H. H. Esser, 2 (1976):594-97; s.v. "ἐργάζομαι," by H. C. Hahn, 3 (1978):1147-52; s.v. "ζωή," by S. Aulen, 2 (1976):44-52; s.v. "θάνατος," by W. Schmithals, 1 (1975):430-41; s.v. "θέλω," by D. Mueller, 3 (1978):1018-23; s.v. "θυμός," by H. Schonweiss, 1 (1975):105-6; s.v. "ἰσχύς," by G. Braumann, 3 (1978):712-14; s.v. "κράτος," by G. Braumann, 3 (1978):716-18; s.v. "καλέω," by L. Coenen, 1 (1975):271-76; s.v. "κτίσις," by H. H. Esser, 1 (1975):378-87; s.v. "μακροθυμία," by V. Falkenroth and C. Brown, 2 (1976):768-72; s.v. "οἰκτιρμός," by H. H. Esser, 2 (1976):598; s.v. "ὀργή," by H. C. Hahn, 1 (1975):107-13; s.v. "πείθομαι," by O. Michel, 1 (1975):588-605; s.v. "προγινώσκω," by P. Jacobs and H. Krienke, 1 (1975):692-93; s.v. "προορίζω," by P. Jacobs and H. Krienke, 1 (1975):695-96; s.v. "προτίθημι," by P. Jacobs and H. Krienke, 1 (1975): 696-97; s.v. "σοφία," by C. Brown, 3 (1978):1026-33; s.v. "φθείρω," by F. Merkel, 1 (1975):467-70; s.v. "χρηστός," by E. Beyreuther, 2 (1976):105-7.

Nielson, Charles Merritt. "More or Less Grace." The Journal of Bible and Religion 30 (July 1962):232-36.

O'Collins, Gerald G. "Power Made Perfect in Weakness." Catholic Biblical Quarterly 33 (October 1971):528-37.

Reese, James M. "Christ as Wisdom Incarnate: Wiser Than Solomon, Loftier Than Lady Wisdom." Biblical Theology Bulletin 11 (April 1981):44-47.

________. "Paul Proclaims the Wisdom of the Cross." Biblical Theology Bulletin 9 (October 1979):147-53.

Reumann, John. "The Gospel of the Righteousness of God." Interpretation 20 (October 1966):432-52.

Riviere, W. T. "The God of Mercy." The Evangelical Quarterly 6 (1934):87-88.

Rupes, James H. "'Righteousness,' and 'The Righteousness of God' in the Old Testament and in St. Paul." Journal of Biblical Literature 22 (1903):211-27.

Sanday, W. "Some Leading Ideas in the Theology of St. Paul." The Expositor 1:8 (1878):40-58.

Scheef, Richard L., Jr. "The Power of God in the Gospel." Theology and Life 6 (Winter 1963):298-308.

Suchook, Marjorie. "The Question of Immortality." The Journal of Religion 57 (July 1977):288-306.

Thayer's Greek-English Lexicon of the New Testament. By Joseph Henry Thayer.

Theological Dictionary of the New Testament. Edited by Gerhard Kittel and Gerhard Friedrich. Translated and edited by Geoffrey W. Bromiley. 1964-74. S.v. "ἀγαπάω," by Ethelbert Stauffer, 1 (1964):35-55; s.v. "ἀίδιος," by Hermann Sasse, 1 (1964):168; s.v. "ἀθανασία," by Rudolph Bultmann, 3 (1965):22-25; s.v. "αἰών, αἰώνιος," by Hermann Sasse, 1 (1964):197-209; s.v. "ἀλήθεια, ἀληθής, ἀληθινός, ἀληθεύω," by Rudolph Bultmann, 1 (1964):232-51; s.v. "ἀνέχω, ἀνεκτός, ἀνοχή," by Heinrich Schlier, 1 (1964):359-60; s.v. "ἀπτομία," by Helmut Köster, 8 (1972):106-9; s.v. "ἀψευδής," by Hans Conzelmann, 9 (1974):594-603; s.v. "βούλομαι, βουλή, βούλημα," by Gottlob Schrenk, 1 (1964):629-37; s.v. "γινώσκω," by Rudolph Bultmann, 1 (1964);689-714; s.v. "δίκαιος, δικαιοσύνη, δικαιόω," by Gottlob Schrenk, 2 (1964):182-219; s.v. "δόξα," by Gerhard Kittel and G. von Rad, 2 (1964):233-53; s.v. "δύναμαι, δυνατός, δυνατέω, ἀδυνατός, ἀδυνατέω, δύναμις, δυνάστης, δυναμόω, ενδυναμόω," by Walter Grundmann, 2 (1964):284-317; s.v. "ἐκλέγομαι, ἐκλογή, ἐκλεκτός," by Gottlob Schrenk, 4 (1967):144-92; s.v. "ἔλεος," by Rudolph Bultmann, 2 (1964):477-87; s.v. "ἐκδικέω, ἔκδικος, ἐκδίκησις," by Gottlob Schrenk, 2 (1964): 442-46; s.v. "ἐνεργέω, ἐνέργεια, ἐνέργημα, ἐνεργής," by Georg Bertram, 2 (1964):652-54; s.v. "εὐδοκέω, εὐδοκία," by Gottlob Schrenk, 2 (1964):738-51; s.v. "ζάω, ζωή," by Rudolph Bultmann, Gerhard von Rad, and

Georg Bertram, 2 (1964):832-72; s.v. "θέλω, θέλημα," by Gottlob Schrenk, 3 (1965):44-62; s.v. "θυμός," by Hermann Buchsel, 3 (1965):167-68; s.v. "ἱκανός, ἱκανότης, ἱκανόω," by Karl Rengsterf, 3 (1965):293-96; s.v. "ἰσχύω, ἰσχυρός, ἰσχύς, κατισχύω," by Walter Grundmann, 3 (1965):397-402; s.v. "καλέω, κλῆσις, κλητός," by K. C. Schmidt, 3 (1965):487-96; s.v. "κράτος," by Wilhelm Michaelis, 3 (1965):905-10; s.v. "κτίζω, κτίσις," by Werner Foerster, 3 (1965):1000-1035; s.v. "μακροθυμία, μακροθυμέω, μακρόθυμος, μακροθύμως," by Johannes Hurst, 4 (1967):374-87; s.v. "οἶδα," by Heinrick Seesemann, 5 (1967):116-19; s.v. "οἰκτίρω, οἰκτιρμός, οἰκτίρμων," by Rudolph Bultmann, 5 (1967):159-61; s.v. "ὀργή," by Gustav Stahlin, Oskar Grether, Johannes Fichtner, Hermann Martin Kleinknecht, Otto Procksch, and Erik Sjoberg, 5 (1967): 382-447; s.v. "πίστις, πιστός," by Rudolph Bultmann, 6 (1968):174-223; s.v. "προγινώσκω," by Rudolph Bultmann, 1 (1964):715-16; s.v. "προορίζω," by K. L. Schmidt, 5 (1967):456; s.v. "προσωποληψία," by Edward Lohse, 6 (1968):779-80; s.v. "προτίθημι, πρόθεσις," by Christian Maurer, 8 (1972):164-68; s.v. "σοφία," by Ulrich Wilckens and Georg Fohrer, 7 (1971):465-526; s.v. "φθείρω," by Gunther Harder, 9 (1974):93-106; s.v. "χάρις, χάρισμα, χαρίζομαι, χαριτόω," by Hans Conzelmann, 9 (1974):372-406; s.v. "χρηστός, χρηστότης," by Konrad Weiss, 9 (1974):483-91.

A Theological Word Book of the Bible. Edited by Alan Richardson, 1962 ed. S.v. "Authority," by J. V. Campbell, pp. 26-27; s.v. "Call, called, calling," by J. P. Thornton-Duesbery, pp. 39-40; s.v. "Chose, chosen, elect, election," by N. H. Snaith, pp. 43-44; s.v. "Determinate, determine, predestinate, foreordain," by J. K. S. Reid, pp. 64-68; s.v. "Folly, fool, foolish, foolishness," by A. Richardson, pp. 84-85; s.v. "Forbear, forbearance," by N. H. Snaith, p. 85; s.v. "God, gods," by O. S. Rankin, pp. 89-99; s.v. "Good," by E. C. Blackman, pp. 99-100; s.v. "Grace," by N. H. Snaith, pp. 100-102; s.v. "Kind, kindness," by N. H. Snaith, p. 119; s.v. "Know, knowledge," by E. C. Blackman, pp. 121-22; s.v. "Life, live, living," by F. J. Taylor, pp. 127-28; s.v. "Longsuffering," by N. H. Snaith, p. 130; s.v. "Love, lover, lovely, beloved, charity," by C. E. B. Cranfield, pp. 131-36; s.v. "Mercy," by N. H. Snaith, pp. 143-44; s.v. "Patience," by R. Gregor Smith, pp. 164-65; s.v. "Presence, Sanctuary, face, countenance, ark, cloud, glory (shekinah)," by L. H. Brockington, pp. 172-76; s.v. "Providence," by A. M. Ramsey, pp. 182-83; s.v. "Purpose," by O. S. Rankin, pp. 183-84; s.v. "Righteous, righteousness," by N. H. Snaith, pp. 202-4;

s.v. "Time, season," by John Marsh, pp. 258-67; s.v. "Truth," by E. C. Blackman, pp. 269-70; s.v. "Wise, wisdom," by E. C. Blackman, pp. 282-83; s.v. "Wrath, anger, indignation," by N. H. Snaith, pp. 289-90.

Theron, D. J. "Ἀλήθεια in the Pauline Corpus." The Evangelical Quarterly 26 (January 1954):3-18.

The Vocabulary of the Greek Testament: Illustrated from the Papyri and Other Non-Literary Sources. By James Hope Moulton and George Milligan.

Walaskay, Paul W. "Mapping the Brain: A Pathway to God?" Christian Century 96 (March 1977):246-49.

Warfield, Benjamin B. "The Terminology of Love in the New Testament." The Princeton Theological Review 16 (January 1918):1-95.

________. "The Terminology of Love in the New Testament." The Princeton Theological Review 16 (April 1918): 153-203.

Watson, Nigel M. "Simplifying the Righteousness of God: A Critique of J. C. O'Neill's Romans." Scottish Journal of Theology 30 (1977):453-69.

Williams, Sam K. "The 'Righteousness of God' in Romans." Journal of Biblical Literature 99 (June 1980): 241-90.

Wuest, Kenneth S. "Four Greek Words for Love." Bibliotheca Sacra 116 (July-September 1959):241-48.

Zondervan Pictorial Bible Encyclopedia of the Bible. Edited by Merrill C. Tenney. 5 vols. S.v. "Calling, call," by C. H. Horne, 1:694; s.v. "Elect, election," by J. Murray, 2:270-74; s.v. "Eternal," by E. M. Blaiklock, 2:380-81; s.v. "Faith, faithfulness," by R. E. Nixon, 2:479-91; s.v. "Forebearance," by S. Barabas, 2:488-89; s.v. "Foreknow, foreknowledge," by J. Murray, 2:590-93; s.v. "Glory," by M. R. Gordon, 2:730-35; s.v. "Grace," by H. D. McDonald, 2:799-804; s.v. "Good, goods," by S. Barabas, 2:775-76; s.v. "Immortality," by N. Shepherd, 3:262-64; s.v. "Kindness," by R. E. Perry, 3:794-95; s.v. "Life," by W. B. Willis, 3:927-32; s.v. "Longsuffering," by R. E. Perry, 3:958-59; s.v. "Love," by G. B. Funderburk, 3:989-96; s.v. "Mercy," by C. E. Armerding, 4:188-90; s.v. "Omnipresence," by A. H. Leitch, 4:531-32; s.v. "Patience," by R. A. Killen, p. 619; s.v. "Power," by G. R. Lewis, 4:830-32; s.v. "Righteousness," by

A. H. Leitch, 5:104-18; s.v. "Sovereignty of God," by H. B. Kuhn, 5:498-99; s.v. "Truth," by A. F. Holmes, 5:827-29; s.v. "Will," by A. F. Holmes, 5:931-33; s.v. "Wisdom," by H. L. Drumright, 5:939-45; s.v. "Wrath," by W. White, 5:990-95.

Unpublished Materials

Andrus, Joel T. "The Doctrine of God in Johannine Theology." Th.M. thesis, Dallas Theological Seminary, 1968.

Bradley, Duncan Lee. "All the Attributes of God: A Study in Method." Ph.D. dissertation, Southern Illinois University, 1972.

Feinberg, Paul David. "The Doctrine of God in the Pentateuch." Th.D. dissertation, Dallas Theological Seminary, 1968.

Hedge, Vernon C. "The Pauline Concept of the Wrath of God." Th.M. thesis, Dallas Theological Seminary, 1972.

Lindberg, David Robert. "The Pauline Concept of Wisdom." Th.M. thesis, Dallas Theological Seminary, 1947.

Parker, George G. "The Doctrine of God in Habakkuk." Th.M. thesis, Dallas Theological Seminary, 1950.

Petersen, Gordon E. "The Doctrine of God in the Book of James." Th.M. thesis, Dallas Theological Seminary, 1970.

Rammel, John George. "The Doctrine of God in Amos." Th.M. thesis, Dallas Theological Seminary, 1955.

Wiedman, Stanley R. "An Exegetical Study of the Wrath of God in the New Testament." Th.M. thesis, Dallas Theological Seminary, 1978.

Wire, Antoinette Clark. "Pauline Theology as an Understanding of God: The Explicit and the Implicit." Ph.D. dissertation, Claremont Graduate School, 1974.

Made in the USA
Monee, IL
04 January 2024

51134760R00111